Lives He Touched

Lives He Touched

The Relationships of Jesus

DAVID A. REDDING

1817

Published in San Francisco by Harper & Row, Publishers

New York, Hagerstown, San Francisco, London

FIRST EDITION

Designed by Jim Mennick

International Standard Book Number: 0-06-066815-6
Library of Congress Catalog Card Number: 77-20443

78 79 80 81 82 10 9 8 7 6 5 4 3 2 1

This book is dedicated to

DORIS WOODS CARY,

Beloved godmother to our children,
Always my wise counselor and copy editor,
My wife's best friend and
An incomparable angel to our family
Ever since she chaired the pulpit committee
That welcomed us to our first home.
She has always been our beautiful, Do,
And she has never failed to bring us joy.
I feel in my heart that she is one of the
Lives He touched.

Acknowledgements

Dorothy McCleery Redding
Doris Woods Cary
Velma Young Pierce

Contents

EVERY year at the Passover festival, Jesus' parents used to go to Jerusalem. When he was twelve years old they went up to the city as usual for the festival. When it was over they started back home, but the boy Jesus stayed behind in Jerusalem, without his parents' knowledge. They went a day's journey assuming that he was somewhere in their company, and then they began to look for him among their relations and acquaintances. They failed to find him, however, and turned back to the city, looking for him as they went. Three days later, they found him—in the Temple, sitting among the teachers, listening to them and asking them questions. All those who heard him were astonished at his powers of comprehension and at the answers that he gave. When Joseph and Mary saw him, they could hardly believe their eyes, and his mother said to him,

"Why have you treated us like this, my son? Here have your father and I been worried, looking for you everywhere!"

And Jesus replied,

"But why were you looking for me? Did you not know that I must be in my Father's house?"

But they did not understand his reply. Then he went home with them to Nazareth and was obedient to them. And his mother treasured all these things in her heart. And as Jesus continued to grow in body and mind, he grew also in the love of God and of those who knew him.

—LUKE 2:41–52, *Phillips*

1 / Jesus' Relationship with His Mother

No one in the Bible tells us anything about Jesus as a boy except Luke, and he allows us only a tantalizing glimpse. We can thank the evangelists for leaving out all that was not gospel.

One is shocked at the superstition manufactured in the Apocrypha. The Gospel of Thomas distorts Jesus' home life, portraying him as a petulant elf carrying spilt water in a robe, stretching boards to double their length, and pulling different colored cloths from the same vat of dye. Such fiction makes out Jesus to be a young monster who insults Joseph and strikes playmates dead for crossing him. A glance at such yarns proves how wise Isaiah was to say, "He shall grow up before him as a tender plant, and as a root out of dry ground" (Isaiah 53:2, KJV). After all, the biblical writers were not compiling a nostalgic scrapbook of childhood memories, but were crowning Him the once and future King. They did not have time to go into the boy's life, for this man must save the world.

They were not writing the life *of* Christ, but the life *in* Christ.

However, there are telling illustrations of how he got along with people. Those having to do with miracles or parables I have presented in other volumes. This book presents twelve personal contacts, beginning with his mother.

Other than the nativity scene, there is only one picture of Jesus' home life from his early years. In his second chapter, Luke catches Christ in what appears at first to be an act of juvenile delinquency. It involves the generation gap and the parents backing down.

After Jesus' birth, Joseph and Mary did not leave Bethlehem until they had "performed everything according to the law . . ." (Luke 2:39, RSV). Jesus was a Jew descended from David and obviously was reared as one. According to Luke, Jesus was properly circumcised, and his parents paid the minimum pair of doves or pigeons since they were too poor to buy a lamb. Jesus would later unearth his great commandment from its burial place, as we learn from Leviticus and Deuteronomy. He and his apostles would go to the synagogue as long as they could. And when they were thrown out they would take with them all the law and the prophets.

The holy family "returned into Galilee, to their own city, Nazareth" (Luke 2:39, RSV). Galilee, which means circle, refers to a province of twenty cities that Solomon paid King Hiram of Tyre in return for cedar timber. Hiram cursed Galilee as "disgusting." That poverty pocket has always been despised as the home of ignorant hillbillies,

"Galilee of the Gentiles" (Matthew 4:15, JBP). It is stigmatized to this day as the poorest and unworthiest place imaginable.

Mary and Joseph settled there in their home town, Nazareth. Nazareth was not much even in Galilee. It was never even mentioned in the Old Testament or the Talmud. Nathanael's famous last words are still repeated: "Can anything good come out of Nazareth?" (John 1:46, Phillips). But if that village had no names to drop, nor any famous schools, the tourist will testify to this day that it offers a magnificent view of snowcapped Mt. Hermon and Mt. Carmel, where Elijah stood alone against Queen Jezebel and her priests. Figs, olives, and pomegranates still grow in groves hedged by cactus. And for a few weeks in the spring the dismal countryside is blanketed with wild flowers. The town also has good water, which comes from what has been called for centuries, "The Virgin's Well," honoring that town's most influential Jewish mother.

Jesus' home was not as fancy as depicted in Fra Angelico's painting. No doubt doves roosted on the flat-roofed house and sandals lined the doorway. The only ornament inside was a light hanging from the ceiling. There were some water jars standing on the floor, and in the corner some sleeping mats and quilts. The family probably ate from a large tray placed on a painted stool. Perhaps there was a brightly colored wooden chest containing all the family valuables.

Luke neglected to tell us what Joseph did for a living, but Matthew mentioned someone's ridicule: "Is not this the carpenter's son?" (Matt. 13:55, RSV). Like many things that were said to hurt, this has helped us to know Jesus better. It means Jesus was at first underfoot with Joseph as much as with Mary, for his shop would have been inside or at the side of the house. No doubt Jesus learned some things working with wood and stone that would later work with men. His father was never mentioned again after the incident in the temple, so it is generally assumed that Joseph must have died soon after, leaving Jesus, as the eldest son of a large family, head of the house. Joseph and Jesus must have been close, for Jesus affectionately chose the word *Father* as his favorite name for God. Joseph is very much a part of his son's life through Jesus' decisive experience of manhood, his trip to Jerusalem for his twelfth Passover.

"And the child grew and became strong, filled with wisdom; and the favor of God was upon him" (Luke 2:40, RSV). He was not a sickly child, and no doubt because of the grim necessities of a builder's family then he matured early.

His Jewish education was profound, if domestic. The ancient historian Flavius Josephus said, "Young Jews knew their laws as well as they knew their own names." Every Sabbath Jesus went to the synagogue where within four years he would hear enough verses read to cover all the law and the prophets. It was read first in Hebrew, then translated into his native tongue of Aramaic. Jesus excelled. He staggered the professors in the temple when he was twelve and stumped the experts to the end of his life.

"Every year at the Passover festival, Jesus' parents used to go to Jerusalem. When he was twelve years old they went up to the city as usual . . ." (Luke 2:41–42, Phillips). It was different this time for he was twelve. This birthday, and the bar mitzvah that would take place that year, moved him from the women's to the men's side of the synagogue. As the star over the stable symbolized he was God's Son, this trip to Jerusalem signified his manhood.

"When [the celebration] was over they started back home, but the boy Jesus stayed behind in Jerusalem, without his parents' knowledge. They went a day's journey assuming that he was somewhere in their company . . ." (Luke 2:43–44, Phillips). The family's casualness confesses not carelessness so much as confidence in him. It also reveals a relaxation of Mary's hold on Christ. A possessive mother would not have permitted that much time to pass before touching base with her firstborn son.

When Joseph and Mary finally found Jesus, Mary scolded him: "Why have you treated us like this, my son? Here have your father and I been worried, looking for you everywhere!" (Luke 2:48, Phillips). It is surprising that young Jesus did take off for three days without an explanation. And even when they found him three days later he had not yet started home nor sent any message; he was still arresting the teachers with his brilliance. How many parents today would take a three-day absence so lightly? That was a serious infraction then as now.

It is strange that Mary should speak ahead of Joseph. In fact, she speaks to Jesus for Joseph. According to the Bible, Joseph never says a word. But they seem such human parents, bewildered by Jesus' seeming disobedience. They sweep away the years between us by the trouble they have communicating with their adolescent son. They have been looking everywhere for him for days and nights. How could he do this to them?

It would be a mistake to interpret this situation as unique to our Saviour. The Bible was written about Jesus; by reading carefully we can see how a boy becomes a man.

Jesus is not apologetic. He questions his parents: "Why were you looking for me? Did you not know that I must be in my Father's house?" (Luke 2:49, Phillips). Jesus is really saying: "I am not your little boy anymore. Now I belong to God." Jesus differed with his parents and won the argument. This temple incident not only testifies to his wisdom with the professors, but to his new relationship with his parents. After that incident he was treated not as an eight-year-old but as a teenager.

"But they did not understand his reply" (Luke 2:50, Phillips). Can parents ever accept a child suddenly becoming an adult? Overnight this child they have been diapering and tucking in at night has quit asking for another glass of water and comes down the stairs taller than his parents, rumbling good morning in a bass voice. This forces an almost impossible adjustment on the parents. A father seems like a monarch when that toddler is cribbed upstairs at his say so. But in a few short years the father goes from king to president, then finally to a figurehead.

At the first sign of adolescent rebellion parents may panic into overreacting discipline. That is a grave mistake, but one that Mary and Joseph do not make. Puzzled as they are, they do not shout Jesus down. They do not unman him. Nor do they punish him. They do not force him to apologize, or humiliate him in front of other people.

Jesus goes home with them obediently. He continues graciously under their authority because they recognize he is no longer a little child and because it is the right thing for him to do.

When parents have their first run-ins with adolescent sons or daughters, they should react like drivers do when the road freezes to ice. Apply the brakes and the accelerator very cautiously or they will have the opposite effect. A child must learn discipline at an early age, but teenagers must be treated differently. In order for teenagers to obey happily, they must be recognized as young adults. A new relationship must be negotiated. And if Mary and Joseph had the wisdom to listen to the teenage Christ, so should other parents.

Some firmness must be used in dealing with little children, but very quickly it must give way to trust. The most powerful weapon a father has with a teenage son is to consult with him, to reach an agreement on the right course, and above all for the father to ask his son's advice and forgiveness. Mary and Joseph were not simply showing us how to deal with a young God, but with a young man. Let yours win their wings, their dignity, and their freedom. They must be allowed to differ with you, to win arguments without being rejected. They will love you for it, and then when the time comes for them to be their own man or woman, it will not be such a huge adjustment.

Mary and Joseph knew how to exercise "judicious

neglect," how to exercise their authority humbly and modestly in order to allow their son to grow up, increasing "in wisdom and in stature, and in favor with God and man" (Luke 2:52, RSV).

The fact that Jesus was a good Jew and a poor, remote Galilean might suggest he was a homebody. And since Joseph disappeared so soon, one might wonder if Jesus had been dominated by his mother. But Jesus' attitude in the temple incident indicates the contrary, as do later exchanges between mother and son in the New Testament.

According to the Gospel of John, chapter two, Mary attends a wedding in Cana (the home of Nathanael), also attended by Jesus and his disciples. "When the wine failed, the mother of Jesus said to him, 'They have no wine.' And Jesus said to her, 'O woman, what have you to do with me? My hour has not yet come.' His mother said to the servants, 'Do whatever he tells you'" (John 2:3–5, RSV). Jesus does accede to her request, but his comments to her do not sound as though he is being intimidated. She obviously leaves the decision to him.

Later, during his active ministry, according to Matthew "While he was still speaking to the people, behold, his mother and his brothers stood outside, asking to speak to him. But he replied to the man who told him, 'Who is my mother, and who are my brothers?' And stretching out his hand toward his disciples, he said, 'Here are my mother and my brothers! For whoever does the will of my Father in heaven is my brother, and sister, and mother'" (Matt. 12:46–52, RSV).

This passage confirms that Jesus healthily left his father and mother to cleave to his lifework and his disciples. He is not being disrespectful of Mary in these passages, but he clearly proclaims his independence. Whether she had come to persuade him to give up this strange ministry or to reinvolve him in family business, he demonstrates for every son that he must be his own man under God and not return to being mother's boy.

This does not mean an abandonment of responsibility or love for his mother. To Jews the commandment to "honor thy father and mother" particularly referred to caring for them when they became old. Obviously, Jesus had freed himself from home as he had recommended other men to do. He may even have had to do it in opposition to his mother's wishes, but that did not mean he deserted or excluded her.

One of his seven last words from the cross is devoted to his mother: "Standing by the cross of Jesus were his mother, and his mother's sister, Mary the wife of Clopas, and Mary Magdalene. When Jesus saw his mother, and the disciple whom he loved standing near, he said to his mother, 'Woman, behold, your son!' Then he said to the disciple, 'Behold, your mother!' And from that hour the disciple took her to his own home" (John 19:25–28, RSV).

It is beautiful to discover that Mary was not merely standing by her son at his death. She went to live with his beloved disciple, and in the first chapter of Acts she is obviously one of those who devoutly believes in Him at Pentecost: "All these with one accord devoted themselves to prayer, together with the women and Mary the mother of Jesus, and with his brothers" (Acts 1:14, RSV).

Mary is more than a mother. She becomes a believer. Is that the example? Mary had more to do than rear children. She learned from her children. She went beyond motherhood to a career of faith. Her larger occupation freed him to be Saviour. She gave him up at the cross, as she had done upon conception and in the temple. Mary and Jesus made their relationship a beautiful one for any mother and son to follow.

THE Gospel of Jesus Christ, the Son of God, begins with the fulfilment of this prophecy of Isaiah—

> Behold, I send my messenger before thy face,
> Who shall prepare thy way;
> The voice of one crying in the wilderness,
> Make ye ready the way of the Lord,
> Make his paths straight.

For John came and began to baptize men in the desert, proclaiming baptism as the mark of a complete change of heart and of the forgiveness of sins. All the people of the Judaean countryside and everyone in Jerusalem went out to him in the desert and received his baptism in the river Jordan, publicly confessing their sins.

John himself was dressed in camel-hair, with a leather belt round his waist, and he lived on locusts and wild honey. The burden of his preaching was, "There is someone coming after me who is stronger than I—indeed I am not good enough to kneel down and undo his shoes. I have baptised you with water, but he will baptize you with the Holy Spirit."

—MARK 1:1–8, *Phillips*

2 / His Best Man

John the Baptist was like a twin brother to Christ. After Mary, John appears to be closest to Jesus' affection and plans. No one can know for certain so private a matter, for Saint John was "the other disciple whom Jesus loved" (John 20:2), to say nothing of Peter, James, Andrew, and Lazarus. However, John the Baptist was Jesus' cousin and possibly his childhood playmate. Before the two boys were born their families were informed by an angel that they were partners in glory as well as blood. Jesus and John would both be murdered young for preaching.

Before Gabriel came to tell Mary about her pregnancy, he visited her cousin Elizabeth's husband, Reverend Zechariah, to tell him that his childless wife would have a boy named John. The angel struck the old preacher speechless for not believing it.

Six months later, when Gabriel reached Mary with the news of Jesus, he told her that her old relative Elizabeth was about to give birth to a son, John.

Mary hurried to Elizabeth. As soon as Elizabeth saw Mary she felt life and cried in consternation: "Why is this granted me, that the mother of my lord should come to me? (Luke 1:43, RSV). What would anyone think over-hearing these two expectant mothers shouting for joy, thrown into each other's arms? Jesus and John were bound inseparably even before they were born.

John's father sent out a little birth announcement, confirming this opening in the family business, which awaited John. Jesus would depend on John to sound the alert: "And you, child," said the old man, "will be called the prophet. . . . You will go before the Lord to prepare . . ." (Luke 1:76, RSV).

"And the child grew and became strong in spirit, and he was in the wilderness till the day of his [debut in] Israel" (Luke 1:80, RSV). That wilderness was John's campus. Men now smile at such academic deprivation. We pity that poor man who matriculated among the stones and cactus without the benefit of city water and all the marvelous influences that had been the rage in towns like Sodom and Gomorrah. As spartan as his isolation was, John enjoyed the luxury of the silent night and an unobstructed view. Away from the noise of traffic one gains time to think of God. A burning bush stands out there. John could never be bundled in an Oxford cap and gown. His God escaped a corrupted temple.

The Lord wants us to hear neither the voice of the television commercial, nor the voice of what "others are saying." The Lord protected John from the diseases of society. He attended a private school no one had heard of. God tutored him so that men dying in the city could hear before it was too late the uncontaminated "voice of one crying in the wilderness . . ." (Mark 1:3, Phillips).

No wonder then that "in the fifteenth year of the reign of Tiberius Caesar, Pontius Pilate being governor of Judea, and Herod being tetrarch of Galilee, and his brother Philip tetrarch of the region of Ituraea and Trachonitis, and Lysanias was tetrarch of Abilene, in the high-priesthood of Annas and Caiaphas, the word of God came to John . . ." (Luke 3:1–2, RSV).

John was different from Jesus. "Now John was clothed with camel's hair, and had a leather girdle around his waist, and ate locusts and wild honey" (Mark 1:6, RSV). John was not Presbyterian, nor a wedding goer; he lived in the desert. John was as different from Jesus as an Amishman is from an Episcopalian. Yet they were dear to each other. John ate locusts and preached repentance. Jesus never accused John of antisocial behavior. Can you imagine any individuals further apart than this hermit and the One who called himself a bridegroom and allowed women to wash his feet? Yet they never tried to change each other.

Many men who think of themselves as tolerant and liberal would have scorned John. No Pharisee or fastidious professor wants to have a man like John around, preaching the wrath to come. They'll hire someone who agrees with and dresses like them.

Jesus and John shared common feelings about God and his kingdom, so they could afford the luxury of being themselves and enjoying the things that distinguished them. They were to do different jobs, reach different audiences, see different sides, and be themselves in service of the same God. "John the baptizer appeared in the wilderness, preaching . . ." (Mark 1:4, RSV); Jesus came preaching (Mark 1:38, paraphrase). Preaching was another bond between them. Paul called it "the foolishness of preaching" (I Cor. 1:21, KJV).

Both John and Jesus stayed out of politics. They were neither radicals nor revolutionists, as some may think. "Tax collectors also came to be baptized, and said to [John], 'Teacher, what shall we do?' And he said to them, 'Collect no more than is appointed you.' Soldiers also asked him, 'And we, what shall we do?' And he said to them, 'Rob no one by violence or by false accusation, and be content with your wages' " (Luke 3:12–14, RSV).

John, however, was rough as a preacher. His sermons were not varied by parables nor relieved by the paradox and compassion of Christ. Both of them hated pharisaism, and John was at his best blasting away at it. They swarmed to the Jordan to hear him, and he let them have it: "You brood of vipers! Who warned you to flee from the wrath to come? Bear fruits that befit repentance, and do not begin to say to yourselves, 'We have Abraham as our father'; for I tell you, God is able from these stones to raise up children to Abraham" (Luke 3:7–8, RSV).

The fact that they were itinerant and uneducated preachers certainly alienated Jesus and John from certain people, including many clergymen of the time. The two were carrying out a very lonely operation.

Jesus felt that he and John offered the people two approaches to God, but most people rejected both of them. Jesus cried: "To what shall I compare this generation? It is like children sitting in the market places and calling to their playmates, 'We piped to you, and you did not dance; we wailed, and you did not mourn.' For John came neither eating nor drinking, and they say, 'He has a demon'; the Son of man came eating and drinking, and they say, 'Behold, a glutton and a drunkard, a friend of tax collectors and sinners!' Yet wisdom is justified by her deeds" (Matt. 11:16–19, RSV). The Living Bible has it: "But brilliant men like you can justify your every inconsistency."

Jesus and John were not simply alone in the world; except for each other they were failures. "He came unto his own, and his own received him not" (John 1:11, KJV).

Jesus and John thought the world of each other. Jesus could have cut John down to "number two" since the crowds lashed out at John, but Jesus may have joined John's crowds at first. How could Jesus have recommended John any more highly? Recalling the crowds who came to hear John preach, Christ said: "When you went out to John in the desert what did you expect to see? A blade of grass bending in the wind, . . . a man dressed up in fancy clothes . . . a prophet? Yes, I tell you—you saw much more than a prophet. For John is the one of whom the Scripture says: 'Here is my messenger, says God. I will send him ahead of you to open the way for you.' Remember this! John the Baptist is greater than any man who ever lived. But he who is least in the kingdom of heaven is greater than he . . . All the prophets and the Law of Moses, until the time of John, spoke about the Kingdom; and if you are willing to believe their message, John is

Elijah" (Matt. 11:7–14, TEV). Here Jesus paid John the highest tribute. Jesus declared that John was foretold in the Bible. Then instead of Jesus honoring John by letting John be the first man Jesus ever baptized, "Jesus came from Galilee to the Jordan to John, to be baptized by him" (Matt. 3:13, RSV).

John's attitude toward Jesus is one of the most beautiful things in history. People were pouring out of Jerusalem to hear John. Very important persons wanted him to baptize them. "And all men questioned in their hearts concerning John, whether perhaps he were the Christ ..." (Luke 3:15, RSV). Most men could not have handled such adulation. It would have gone to their heads:

"John, aren't you the one? Just look at that crowd?"

"Well perhaps I am."

To the contrary John's head was never turned by that heady popularity. He answered: "I baptize you with water; but he who is mightier than I is coming, the thong of whose sandals I am not worthy to untie; he will baptize you with the Holy Spirit and with fire" (Luke 3:16, RSV).

When Jesus, who was John's junior in the ministry, went to John to be baptized, John could have paternally told him, "Son, you'll go far, but I have seniority. Since I'm six months older and have been a member longer, I should baptize you." Not at all. John didn't feel equal to baptizing Christ. "John would have prevented him, saying, 'I need to be baptized by you, and do you come to me?' But Jesus answered him, 'Let it be so now; for thus it is fitting for us to fulfil all righteousness.' Then he consented. And when Jesus was baptized, he went up immediately from the water, and behold, the heavens were opened and he saw the Spirit of God descending like a dove, and alighting on him; and lo, a voice from heaven, saying, 'This is my beloved Son, with whom I am well pleased' " (Matt. 3:14–17, RSV).

That would not have been possible without John's humility. He received no medals. He wanted nothing for himself. Comparing himself to Christ, John said, "He must increase, but I must decrease" (John 3:30, RSV). What a man! Have you ever rejoiced about a friend's superiority over you?

On one occasion John said that he did not know who Jesus was, and later from prison just before his death he inquired of Jesus: "Are you he who is to come, or shall we look for another?" (Matt. 11:3, RSV). This is puzzling. Perhaps John was humanly bewildered by continually discovering that his best friend was the Son of God. Perhaps he was also puzzled by the way things were working out. But earlier when Jesus walked by, John the Baptist, without hesitation, declared: "Behold, the Lamb of God, who takes away the sin of the world!" (John 1:29, RSV).

John surely inspired Jesus by his courage. While John did not meddle in politics, he would not hesitate to call a king on any misbehavior. He condemned Herod Antipas for getting rid of his own wife and stealing Herodias, the wife of his half-brother Philip. Antipas arrested John for this and imprisoned him in a castle by the Dead Sea. At Antipas's birthday party Herodias figured out a way to get John. Herodias's daughter Salomé performed a lascivious dance for the birthday celebration. Antipas was so pleased that he recklessly promised Salomé anything she wanted as her reward. Prompted by her mother Herodias, Salomé declared: "I want you to give me at once the head of John the Baptist on a platter" (Mark 6:25, RSV).

When news of this horrible thing reached Jesus it is said "he withdrew . . . to a lonely place apart" (Matt. 14:13, RSV). It must have broken Jesus' heart, and it must have made him determined not to let John down. Jesus' best friend had paid the price to open the way for him.

God only knows, as Jesus walked down that path, how much John's life and death meant to him. Truly John had been the one to baptize Christ and to accompany him as far as he could.

"You yourselves can witness that I said, 'I am not Christ but I have been sent as his forerunner.' It is the bridegroom who possesses the bride, yet the bridegroom's friend who merely stands and listens to him can be overjoyed to hear the bridegroom's voice. That is why my happiness is now complete' " (John 3:28–29, Phillips).

JESUS returned from the Jordan full of the Holy Spirit and he was led by the Spirit to spend forty days in the desert, where he was tempted by the devil. He ate nothing during that time and afterwards he felt very hungry.

"If you are the Son of God," the devil said to him, "tell this stone to turn into a loaf."

Jesus answered,

"The scripture says, 'Man shall not live by bread alone.' "

Then the devil took him up and showed him all the kingdoms of mankind in a sudden vision, and said to him,

"I will give you all this power and magnificence, for it belongs to me and I can give it to anyone I please. It shall all be yours if you will fall down and worship me."

To this Jesus replied,

"It is written, 'Thou shalt worship the Lord thy God and him only shalt thou serve.' "

Then the devil took him to Jerusalem and set him on the highest pinnacle of the Temple.

"If you are the Son of God," he said, "throw yourself down from here, for the scripture says, 'He shall give his angels charge concerning thee, to guard thee,' and 'On their hands they shall bear thee up, lest haply thou dash thy foot against a stone.' "

To which Jesus replied,

"It is also said, 'Thou shalt not tempt the Lord thy God.' "

And when he had exhausted every kind of temptation, the devil withdrew until his next opportunity.

—LUKE 4:1–13, *Phillips*

3 / His Worst Enemy

Jesus made many enemies. He crossed the Pharisees and Sadducees. They crossed him. Judas betrayed him. Pilate sentenced him. Caiaphas cursed him. Soldiers crammed thorns into the crown of his head. An angry mob tore him with rocks and ridicule. "Were you there when they crucified my Lord?" It was quite a mass effort.

But all these enemies were small compared to the devil's effort to get Christ. The good earth had been robbed from God and was rotting in the robber's clutches. The best way to say it is that one of God's great angels turned on him (Ezekiel 28:12–19, Isaiah 14:12–17, paraphrase). Jesus' assignment was to defeat this fallen angel and to recover all creation.

Jesus was God's champion against Lucifer. It was a battle to the death. "The reason the Son of God appeared was to destroy the works of the devil" (1 John 3:8, RSV).

Jesus must have known about the opposition very early in life, for his Jewish parents would have told him the story in the Old Testament. Adam and Eve no sooner basked in the sunshine of that lovely Eden when in sneaked the serpent, and they were out. And all was lost.

The Bible doesn't explain; it simply portrays the unfolding tragedy. God made the world for good, but it lost its place like a falling star. Instead of enjoying God, Adam and Eve devoured forbidden fruit, and the family of man was soon feverishly at work erecting a tower of Babel from which to look down on their outgrown God.

The pity of it all was never more eloquently put than on the eve of the flood. "And God saw that the wickedness of man was great in the earth, and that every imagination of the thoughts of his heart was only evil continually. And it repented the Lord that he had made man on the earth, and it grieved him at his heart" (Genesis 6:5, KJV).

Jesus was born into this heartbreaking situation. The world was almost beyond hope, waiting, not only for someone to set a good example, but for someone who could break the curse of evil. "We wrestle not against flesh and blood, but against principalities, against powers, against the rulers of the darkness of this world . . . (Eph. 6:12, KJV). An authority was needed, empowered with "the whole armour of God . . . [to] be able to stand against the wiles of the devil" (Eph. 6:11, KJV).

Noah built an ark. Abraham made the Old Testament with God. Moses split the Red Sea, which had imprisoned the Israelites in Egypt. David rehearsed the kingdom. Job became a test between God and the devil. All the law and the prophets played a part in God's program of rehabilitation, but the battle was too great for anything short of God's final Word. Time was up. "God so loved the world, that he gave his only begotten Son, that whosoever believeth in him should not perish . . . (John 3:16, KJV).

The devil was obviously busy early in the life of Christ, for Herod even tried to persuade the Wise Men to reveal the whereabouts of the child. Mary and Joseph were warned in a dream to flee to Egypt with the baby before they were caught in Herod's "massacre of the innocents," which was the old king's desperate attempt to eliminate all competition. While all this is clearly devil's work, the devil does not appear until Jesus leaves his seclusion in Nazareth to be baptized on the banks of the Jordan before John the Baptist.

Immediately after God had blessed Jesus at his baptism, the devil was ready for him, and "Jesus was . . . tempted by the devil" (Matt. 4:1, RSV). We ask, "You don't mean Jesus had trouble keeping his mind on God?" The book of Hebrews confesses that he is: "One who in every respect has been tempted as we are" (Hebrews 4:15, RSV). Being good did not come easy to Christ. The cross was not rigged in his favor. The life of Christ was a struggle to the death.

Men have reduced Christ to a God who automatically grinds out good deeds until many cannot see Jesus pinned down in the flesh. But in his temptation in the wilderness, we are invited to witness Jesus' first encounter with Satan. He did not have a "crib sheet" for his test. He dug out the answers himself for our sake.

Christ's war against the devil makes our moral scuffles seem like child's play. God sent Jesus to the front to lead the attack. We gripe about what we have to give up for oodness sake. He purchased us with a price that could ιot be paid back, and "like a sheep led before his shearers is dumb, so he opened not his mouth" (Isa. 53:7, Acts 8:32, RSV). An Australian aborigine could not conceive of the temptations Moses endured in deciding between the pleasures of an Egyptian palace and the spartan assignment of piloting the Exodus. Since we are not on a level with Jesus, we can scarcely appreciate his trial. We know that he fought on fronts where we have never fought. And we have given up where he would have died first. Like us he was tempted. But we have never been tempted like him.

We could not have lasted in the wilderness to which he was taken. Would we not have starved or sneaked home to warm beds long before the forty days were up? We have not carried our fight to such heights. The devil had scouted this man as the one to nail or lose his empire.

Christ knew more about evil than even the devil. Someone whispers: "Don't swear in front of the preacher." But as C. S. Lewis suggests: "Who knows the devil better? His victim or his victor?" Only the conqueror of evil is expert. We don't consult criminals when we are in trouble. So the church is not a club for easily shocked angels. It is a decontamination center. We don't come to Christ to show off, but in search of help. Those who are well have no need of a physician. Our spire was erected by the veteran ace who "descended into hell" and came back the winner.

"Then Jesus was led up by the Spirit . . . tempted . . ." (Matt. 4:1, RSV). Is it possible that evil could tempt

Christ before he was dry from his baptism? Beelzebub hits hardest when the halo is brightest. Blue Monday. His infernal majesty waits us following Communion, when we think we're strongest. He times his visits to follow in the backwash of God's, so he can have the last word.

C. S. Lewis's Screwtape sat down before the Dove's resting place was cold. He was in a better bargaining position, briefed, better able to smear the contract with the Almighty. "Are you sure it was God? What makes you think this isn't an old wives' tale? Remember your mother always said you had a good imagination. You are not going to let your promising young life be boxed in by that old black myth are you? Come, come, straight-laced will do for old-fashioned women, but you are a very special case. Don't you think a cross is a little high? I can make you a better offer. So much easier." Satan follows hard on God's heels.

Jesus struggled so fiercely he forgot his food for forty days. Or did his fight require that awful fast? At last, when Jesus was starving to death, "the devil said to him, 'If you are the Son of God, command this stone to become bread' " (Luke 4:3, RSV). Lucifer waited until Christ was trembling with weakness, and then let him have it in the pit of his empty stomach. But the tempter stretched the offer, tantalizing Jesus not only with his next meal, but with the respectable prospect of feeding the hungry masses everywhere.

The devil's first proposition sidetracked Christ into fighting famine instead of hell. The proposal was well aimed and well timed, for it was close to Christ's heart.

Jesus was God's son, not the grocer's boy. It takes more than soup to interest men in sharing their soup. Christ would not be cowed into becoming a cosmic cook. He must serve more than mere calories. Men must eat, but they are here not only to eat. Carlyle once said: "Not all the finance ministers, and upholsterers, and confectioners of modern Europe . . . in joint stock company, could make one shoeblack happy above an hour or two" (The Interpreter's Bible, vol. VII, p. 271). "The famished Bedouin," George Buttrick wrote, "finding treasure in the desert, cried: 'Alas, it is only diamonds.' " Men hunger and thirst for righteousness, groaning at their dinner tables, "Alas, it is only bread."

Blaming economics for man's predicament was the Bolshevist blunder. Christ was not callous to the children's cries for milk. But that is only a symptom of the heartbreaking famine of the spirit. Jesus steadied himself and spoke through swollen lips: "It is written, 'Man shall not live by bread alone' " (Luke 4:4, RSV).

Then the devil made his second bid. He showed Christ all the kingdoms of this world: "To you I will give all this authority and their glory; for it has been delivered to me, and I give it to whom I will" (Luke 4:6, RSV).

This temptation was no exaggeration. Christ actually faced this choice. Anyone who has what it takes to be remembered so well for two thousand years could certainly have made a name for himself in a number of ways. He rejected popularity. Imagine his success had he sought it. He was the darling of the crowds, hunted and haunted as a celebrity day and night. Men clamored to crown him.

Many dictators have swept into power with a fraction of his support. The time was ripe, for discontent was rife under Rome. Zealots were frantic for a military messiah. His disciples would root for him to take over as David did. The crowd was waiting there for the word from him that would trigger a rebellion.

This temptation must have been great indeed. What would be wrong with accepting the throne of the ideal republic he would establish? Such a coup d' état could give Palestine her golden age. Christ could put his energy into administration and become another lawgiver like Moses. Then he would be in a position to free the people as well as feed them. He could improve their political condition while raising living standards. How that back-country youth must have longed for tangible work, which would achieve immediate results. How heartbreaking was the alternative God had in mind.

Messiahship was a pity—if he *were* God's Son. Perhaps the baptism was a product of his overworked fancy. Was the dove that descended a coincidence? Who else would believe it? Was God going to make him the laughing stock for all time? Did God exist at all? What transpired out there in the desert? The temptation was real, wasn't it? Thirst nagged Him, as did doubt. Which was worse, the hunger or the questions? He was hounded by the wilderness within him. Jagged rocks and vicious briars tore his clothes. He tore his garment, also. Surely by this time vultures circled overhead. The shadow of the cross fell on him. God did not spoil his only child; he brought him up the hard way.

But there was a catch to the devil's offer. Catlike the tempter watched his prey. "Jesus, you can kneel down to me over here." Jesus had difficulty standing, but he turned his back on the devil's request, responding with words from his childhood: "It is written, Thou shalt worship the Lord thy God, and him only . . ." (Luke 4:8, KJV).

After failing to trip Jesus on the first two attempts, Satan made his most alluring offer, and "took [Jesus] to Jerusalem, and set him on the pinnacle of the temple, and said to him, 'If you are the Son of God, throw yourself down from here; for it is written, 'He will give his angels charge of you, to guard you . . .' " (Luke 4:9–10, RSV).

The devil acted now as if he were beaten, as if to say, "All right. You win. I believe you really are God's Son. Now let everyone else in on it too. Jump off this high place. God will help *you* down easily. This will capture everyone's attention and allegiance in one stroke." Then to cast his lure a little more enticingly, Satan got off a line or two of scripture himself.

Men still cannot find the holes in this one. What harm is there in soliciting believers by acrobatics? Something sensational is needed to inspire faith. The devil dared Christ to place himself in peril, so people could see God hurry to his rescue. Satan was attempting to trick the Almighty into exposing himself.

Jesus admitted his fascination with this idea; he was tempted by it. Remember, he was an unknown and unlettered carpenter. How could Christ influence the world without some prop similar to Moses' staff-into-snake trick, which had influenced a Pharoah? His family would

fear he was losing his mind if he spoke about what transpired. He had had forty days of this. How much more
could he take?

But Jesus knew better. People do not become believers
by gymnastics. A magician has no followers except those
he hires. No jump that Christ could take would persuade
anyone to love his neighbor. Jesus could not build his
kingdom on stunts. He reached an astounding conclusion
on how easily people could be influenced: "Neither will
they be persuaded, though one rose from the dead" (Luke
16:31, KJV).

As that grueling match with the fiend ground on, the
thing that saved Christ was the word of God. The devil
could not talk him out of what God had preached. In the
last crucial round Jesus defended himself again with these
words from his heart: "It is said, Thou shalt not tempt the
Lord thy God" (Luke 4:12, KJV).

Then the devil retreated until his next opportunity.
Although Christ had driven off Satan, he would continue
to dog him until the end. "Then the devil left him, and
behold angels came and ministered to him" (Matthew
4:11, RSV). Temptation is no disgrace. God awards the
soldier who stands the tempter off. "And Jesus returned
in the power of the Spirit into Galilee . . ." (Luke 4:14,
KJV).

In his first major confrontation with the devil, Christ
was on the defensive. Christ did not get hurt, but neither
did he hurt the devil. However, from now on Christ
would be on the offensive. Jesus would be hurt terribly,
but he would not leave the field until he had mortally
wounded the devil.

The devil is still very much alive to this day. It will take Armageddon itself to finish him off, but thanks to Jesus' blood the devil is doomed. The crucifixion was fatal, not to Christ but to Lucifer.

Jesus detected the devil's hand in his confrontations with the Pharisees. The devil used devout people of the day as his tool to attack Christ. But Jesus was not fooled or frightened. He was fearless as he unmasked those religious leaders as stooges. The devil used them as a perfect screen.

> You are of your father the devil, and your will is to do your father's desires. He was a murderer from the beginning, and has nothing to do with the truth, because there is no truth in him. When he lies, he speaks according to his own nature, for he is a liar and the father of lies. But because I tell the truth, you do not believe me (John 8:44–45, RSV).

Lucifer, not content to merely strengthen the opposition that would finally kill Christ, infiltrated Jesus' headquarters. On one occasion, when Jesus broke the difficult news that He would have to suffer, Peter reassured him: "God forbid, Lord! This shall never happen to you" (Matt. 16:22, RSV).

But Jesus responded, "Get behind me, Satan!" (Matt. 16:23, RSV). It was especially hard for Jesus to bear because the devil had teased him with this temptation before. Why couldn't Christ be king without the cross? But the devil never relented his pressure on that intimate circle of twelve: "The devil had already put the thought of betraying Jesus into the mind of Judas Iscariot . . ." (John 13:2, Phillips).

One of the devil's strategies was to accuse Christ of working for the devil. Just as they had accused John, so the fickle crowd cursed Christ: "You . . . have a demon!" (John 8:48, Phillips). At another point, the Pharisees tried to convince people that Jesus had success with demons because he was one of them.

But Jesus adroitly defended himself: "If Satan cast out Satan, he is divided against himself; how shall then his kingdom stand?" (Matt. 12:26, KJV). There was no end to the devil's deceit. As Paul said, "Even Satan disguises himself as an angel of light" (2 Cor. 11:14, RSV).

Everywhere Jesus went he healed sicknesses that stemmed from Satan. He cast out the demons and foretold the day of victory.

> I was watching and saw Satan fall from heaven like a flash of lightning! It is true that I have given you the power to tread on snakes and scorpions and to overcome all the enemy's power—there is nothing at all that can do you any harm (Luke 10:18–19, Phillips).

After his entrance into Jerusalem that last time, Jesus announced what he would reaffirm in shining raiment after he had risen: "Now the ruler of this world will be overthrown" (John 12:31, TEV).

During his life, Jesus restored the earth to its owner. Though the mop-up remains to be done, the death of Satan is guaranteed, and the lost paradise is now returning. Jesus shouted loudly, "It is finished" (John 19:30, RSV).

As they continued their journey, Jesus came to a village and a woman called Martha welcomed him to her house. She had a sister by the name of Mary who settled down at the Lord's feet and was listening to what he said. But Martha was very worried about her elaborate preparations and she burst in, saying,

"Lord, don't you mind that my sister has left me to do everything by myself? Tell her to come and help me!"

But the Lord answered her,

"Martha, my dear, you are worried and bothered about providing so many things. Only one thing is really needed. Mary has chosen the best part and it must not be taken away from her!"

—LUKE 10:38–42, *Phillips*

4 / Two Women Friends

Jesus' relationship to women was revolutionary. In a stunning upset God's angel did not announce the King's birth to another Adam or Abraham. Instead Gabriel visited a teenage girl. And Mary is much more prominent in Scripture than Joseph. Women related to Jesus in a way that was unique for a bachelor prophet.

"A woman called Martha welcomed him to her house" (Luke 10:38, Phillips). In the New Testament, Jesus never refuses any offers to dinner from women. Martha kept house for her brother Lazarus in a little suburb named Bethany, about two miles out of Jerusalem. Since Martha invited Jesus, it suggests she ran the house as well as looked after it. Her brother and sister also lived there, but Luke says that Martha invited him to *her* home. One wonders if this relates to Lazarus's later illness. Martha might have been a woman with the strength of a battleship. The scene definitely focuses on Martha and Mary.

"She had a sister by the name of Mary . . ." (Luke 10:39, Phillips). Mary is much more than just Martha's sister. She is special to Christ, and though we cannot be sure, Augustine and others identify her as the woman who came in off the streets while Jesus was dining at Simon the Pharisee's house. Before Martha's invitation, Jesus did have an invitation from Simon, a neighbor of Martha's in Bethany. (Matthew and Mark concur that Simon resided in Bethany.)

During dinner at Simon's, in one of the open-air dining rooms of those days, a woman who "lived a sinful life" walked in off the streets. She heard that Jesus was eating in the Pharisee's house, so she "brought an alabaster flask of perfume and stood behind him crying, letting her tears fall on his feet and then drying them with her hair. Then she kissed them and anointed them with the perfume" (Luke 7:37–38, Phillips).

That Jesus would consent to such brazenness literally transported Simon. Simon knew in a minute that Jesus was no prophet; otherwise he would have known what trash was touching him. But Jesus saw through Simon and pinned him down with a parable that explained Jesus' relationship to this scarlet woman. People still cannot believe it.

"Simon, a certain creditor, had two debtors; one owed five hundred denarii, and the other fifty. When they could not pay, he forgave them both. Now which of them will love him more?" (Luke 7:41–42, paraphrase).

Simon answered, "The one, I suppose, to whom he forgave more" (Luke 7:43, paraphrase).

Jesus said to Simon:

> You're right. When I came tonight to your house I couldn't get you to let me in. You didn't greet me, you didn't even give me water to wash my feet. But do you really see this

woman, Simon? She couldn't wait to see me. She started washing my feet with her tears and drying them with her hair. You didn't kiss me once on the cheek; she hasn't stopped kissing my feet. You didn't waste a drop of oil on my head, and she has anointed me with a whole jar of expensive perfume (Luke 7:44–49, paraphrase).

"Therefore I tell you, many as her sins are, they are forgiven, for her love is great; whereas he to whom little is forgiven has but little love." And he said to the woman, "Your sins are forgiven" (Luke 7:49, Moffatt). It was as though Jesus said:

Simon, your sins are not forgiven because you don't know you have any. You are so aware of how much better you are than this woman that you have no idea of how hard it is for God to accept you. So you'll never know her happiness. She knows how much she needed forgiveness. You don't think you need it. You don't know how far you are from God, Simon. Until you do you'll never have much to be thankful for; you'll never have any reason to ask for God's mercy. What did God ever have to do for you as far as you can see?

Whether or not we assume that this woman was Mary —and I think it is very likely—this incident illustrates Jesus' hatred for the religious man's pride in his own moral superiority, and Jesus' admiration for the down and out who admit they need God. To the end of his life, Jesus tried to break down men like Simon who set themselves apart as better than other people.

Jesus loved and defended to the death those broken and humiliated persons like Mary, who recognized their vast need of God and responded in a burst of thanksgiving and joy. Those who thought they automatically deserved the best would never know any joy. Joy is reserved for those who have discovered they have been saved, not by their own hard work but by an undeserved act of God. Jesus is always tough on the invulnerable like Simon. They do not need a Saviour like him. They think they're set already. Jesus is always the tender Saviour to those, like Mary, who have been hurt and come to him for help.

The fact that Martha and Mary are together in the same house makes the story especially interesting. Perhaps the prodigal sister had just returned, and her upright sister Martha had invited Jesus to dinner to thank him for helping Mary shape up. But the fact that they entertained Jesus does distinguish them. While Mary, Martha, and Lazarus were different from the sinners and outcasts who often gathered around Jesus, they were also unlike the rigid religious households that would have locked him out. These three single adults were special to him more than we know.

In the passage where Martha invites him to dinner it says that "she had a sister by the name of Mary, who settled down at the Lord's feet and was listening to what he said" (Luke 10:39, Phillips). Without reading any further, it is obvious that the hair will rise on the back of Martha's neck as soon as she realizes Mary is relaxing with the men while Martha is stuck preparing dinner.

Martha is so upset that she disrupts Jesus' conversation with a blast at Mary in front of everyone. She looms red-faced in the doorway with her apron on, perhaps pointing in Mary's direction with a ladle: "Lord, don't you mind that my sister has left me to do everything by myself? Tell her to come and help me!" (Luke 10:40, Phillips).

An ordinary man, sensing that what was going on in the kitchen would soon have disastrous implications for his appetite, might have said, "Mary, perhaps you had better give Martha a hand with those beans. I didn't realize how late it was." Martha strikes one as the kind of person you had better go along with.

Had Martha been another kind of person, she might have suffered in silence, or slipped in and whispered something in Mary's ear, which the New Testament need never have overheard. Or perhaps she might have appeared in the doorway and made woeful faces and gone "psss't" or beckoned to Mary with her finger. Not Martha. She barges in, bursting with self-importance, breaks up church, and blurts out in exasperation: "Lord, don't you pity poor me alone out there trying to feed this crowd? Mary's run out on me and I've come after her. Send her out."

Would you have crossed that woman if she had been the hostess who had invited you? Jesus immediately rebukes Martha publicly: "Martha, my dear, you are worried and bothered about providing so many things. Only one thing is really needed. Mary has chosen the best part and it must not be taken away from her!" (Luke 10:41–42, Phillips).

Jesus does not quite say "you're not going to take it away from her, Martha," but he emphatically defends

Mary against any tyranny Martha might have had over Mary. Martha tried to expose Mary, but Jesus exposes Martha. Martha tells Jesus, in effect, "You tell her, Lord, I can't do a thing with her." And Jesus replies as if to say, "No, Martha, I'm not going to help you control Mary. God's going to be Mary's boss from now on, not you. Martha, you want Mary out in the kitchen at your feet instead of at mine. It won't do any longer. She will be out to help you shortly, but not because you are throwing your weight around. Martha, you may have driven Mary out of the house before. But no more. This matriarchy you run here is over. Mary will help you, but no longer at your command."

Martha needed to be embarrassed. She ruined Mary's reputation by that wisecrack and yet no one has ever heard Mary's version. For all we know Mary slaved before Jesus' arrival, and Martha is a chronic complainer. Mary's silence doesn't mean she's guilty. Maybe she is being gracious. It is interesting that Jesus compliments Mary and rebukes Martha, though many people would be inclined to take Martha's side.

Jesus is not excusing laziness. No one would call him a man of leisure. He probably took over his father's construction business from his early teens until his late twenties. And can anyone know how much work is involved in being a Saviour? He worked such miracles in three years that we marvel still. His last day's work here was hard on his hands.

But hard work is not the key here. Jesus recommends rest to Martha; she is overdoing. Someone must prepare the food, but she has created a monster. She was making a production out of bread and wine, olives and cheese. What went on in the kitchen distracted her from what transpired with Christ in the next room. She was in competition with Christ. Jesus might have said:

> Martha, you have turned your kitchen stove into an altar. Don't curse us with dinner-time. We would rather not eat if we must bow down to bread. Martha, you have invited me to dinner. I thank you. But now let me invite you to dinner. I have come to liberate you from the kitchen. Mary's engaged in something more important than cooking. We can all do without dinner. No one can do without the love of God. You can't either, Martha. You'll never get to heaven on a sparkling house and your fig jubilee. The fact that Mary is having a good time in the front room is obnoxious to you Martha because you don't know how to relax or receive. Your schedule is rigged too tightly for me to enter your life. Martha, I'll enjoy your dinner. But let me do something for you.

"Jesus loved Martha and her sister and Lazarus" (John 11:5, RSV). Shortly after this Lazarus becomes sick. When the sisters realize he is dying, they send for Jesus. " 'Lord, your friend is very ill.' When Jesus received the message, he said, 'This illness will not end in death; it will bring glory to God—for it will show the glory of the Son of God' " (John 11:4, Phillips). Incredible as it seems to the sisters, Jesus delays his return to allow time for Lazarus's death and burial in order to perform his mightiest miracle.

By the time Jesus arrives, Lazarus had been in the

ground four days. Martha comes on scolding again. "Lord, if you had been here, my brother would not have died" (John 11:22, RSV). Then Martha fetches Mary. When Jesus saw her weeping, realizing what he had put the sisters through, and how dear they had become to him, "Jesus wept" (John 11:35, RSV), as he never did except over Jerusalem.

Jesus went to the tomb, a cave with a stone placed at the entrance. "Take away the stone," Jesus orders. Suddenly it dawns on Martha what he is going to try and she is appalled. He has come back not to pay his respects but to rob the grave. Jesus' failure to come in time as a physician was bad enough, but for him to go in after Lazarus now is madness. He will make a fool of himself forever. She tries her best to stop Jesus: "Lord, by this time there will be an odor, for he has been dead four days" (John 11:39, RSV).

But again Martha cannot stop Jesus. Again he has more planned than she has in mind. He publicly announces Lazarus's return as an accomplished fact even before checking the tomb to see if his prayer is working. He thanks God before Lazarus reappears. "He cried out with a loud voice, 'Lazarus, come out.' The dead man came out, his hands and feet bound with bandages, and his face wrapped with a cloth. Jesus said to them, 'Unbind him, and let him go' " (John 11:43–44, RSV). This miracle gives Martha even more perspective, and leaves her speechless. She has no more complaints to make in the Bible.

This was Christ's most expensive miracle, for according to John, Lazarus's resurrection forced the Jews to kill Christ. "If we let him go on doing this sort of thing we shall have everybody believing in him" (John 11:48, Phillips).

Shortly after, "six days before the Passover," Jesus went to Bethany for dinner for the last time, "and Martha helped serve it" (John 12:2, Good News for Modern Man). It says she "helped." Perhaps Mary had to come out of the kitchen to drag Martha away from Christ's feet. During that dinner, Saint John says, "Mary took a whole pint of very expensive perfume made of nard, poured it on Jesus' feet, and wiped them with her hair . . . until its fragrance filled the house" (John 12:3, Good News for Modern Man). This would have meant a year's wages then. Mary may have done this the first time to give thanks. Christ said that this time she did it for his burial, since he was facing the cross. Judas objected to its not being spent on the poor. It is better than buying milk for the poor, Jesus said, for it is only spilled milk unless one first spills the perfume. Until its fragrance fills the house no Judas will ever do much with the milk money. "Let her alone, let her keep it for the day of my burial. The poor you always have with you, but you do not always have me" (John 12:7–8, RSV).

Helping Christ can be different from helping the poor. I don't believe there is anyone who hasn't given a little milk to the poor, but life is waiting for the reckless splash of our perfume. What have we done that isn't merely a practical help to the poor, but is also something beautiful for Jesus? Jesus was not simply good to Mary and Martha and Lazarus. He was beautiful to them.

Picturing Mary on her knees in this glorious extravagance makes one wish he'd thought of that. But once one sees the extent Jesus went for him in the outpouring of love something will occur to him to do as beautiful as blessed Mary did.

THEN one of the Jewish rulers put this question to him,

"Master, I know that you are good; tell me, please, what must I do to be sure of eternal life?"

"I wonder why you call me good?" returned Jesus. "No one is good—only the one God. You know the commandments—

"Thou shalt not commit adultery.

"Thou shalt not commit murder.

"Thou shalt not steal.

"Thou shalt not bear false witness.

"Honour thy father and thy mother."

"All these," he replied, "I have carefully kept since I was quite young."

And when Jesus heard that, he said to him,

"There is still one thing you have missed. Sell everything you possess and give the money away to the poor, and you will have riches in Heaven. Then come and follow me."

But when he heard this, he was greatly distressed for he was very rich.

And when Jesus saw how his face fell, he remarked,

"How difficult it is for those who have great possessions to enter the kingdom of God! A camel could squeeze through the eye of a needle more easily than a rich man could get into the kingdom of God."

Those who heard Jesus say this, exclaimed,

"Then who can possibly be saved?"

Jesus replied,

"What men find impossible is possible with God."

"Well," rejoined Peter, "we have left all that we ever had and followed you."

And Jesus told them,

"Believe me, nobody has left his home or wife, or brothers

or parents or children for the sake of the kingdom of God, without receiving very much more in this present life—and eternal life in the world to come."

—LUKE 18:18–30, *Phillips*

5 / The Rich Young Ruler

"And as [Jesus] was setting out on a journey, a man ran up and knelt before him and asked him, 'Good teacher, what must I do to inherit eternal life?' " (Mark 10:17, RSV). Matthew said he was young (19:20, RSV). Luke said he was a ruler (18:18, RSV).

Why does this young man rush to Jesus, just as Jesus is leaving town? Had he been battling himself for days whether or not to bother Jesus, then giving in at the last minute? Or was Jesus the first prophet he heard of who specialized in children, as Jesus had just demonstrated in the preceding verses? All his money couldn't buy the love he saw in Jesus. The young man had heavy responsibilities. Perhaps he envied that Jesus traveling without any luggage. Suddenly he wanted a part of this. He rushed to the feet of Jesus.

Don't departures have a way of driving things home? Departures, like little deaths, drive us to do something. The young man heard the farewells: "Goodbye, Jesus. We'll miss you. Thanks for everything. We'll never forget you." Partings often bring tears. Good-byes have a way of bringing feelings to the surface. The young man might never see such a man as Jesus again. The young man was moved. "I can't let him leave like this."

The rich young ruler did not have an appointment. Jesus wasn't fussy or fettered by a schedule. Jesus' most memorable encounters were impromptu. This ruler came running. He was an important person. What would people think about his coming to Jesus instead of Jesus going to him? He had never bowed down to anyone before. This rich man entreated Jesus, "Good Master." Was it flattery or was it the only way he could express: "Jesus, I haven't been able to get you out of my head since I first saw you."

But Jesus called him on it. "Why do you call me good?" (Luke 18:19, RSV). Jesus won't let him get away with those words. "You know that only God is good. If you are going to include me it will cost more. I'm not looking for compliments. I'm looking for men."

Jesus never hurt anyone's feelings except to humble the proud. Remember how Jesus was so deeply moved by the centurion who called him not only good, but too good to come into his house? Jesus never questioned the centurion's compliment. Jesus said he'd never seen faith like that. But the centurion had come to Christ on behalf of his slave. For some reason Jesus is on guard against the young ruler's praise: "Son, I don't think you know what you are getting into."

The young ruler asks him, "What must I do to be sure of eternal life?" (Luke 18:18, Phillips). It's as if he is saying, "Jesus I have just realized that having everything means nothing. My family left me everything, and yet it isn't anything. A thief could take almost all I have at a moment's notice. The rest will soon rust away. It isn't safe and it isn't satisfying. Tell me what to do to find the treasure 'rust and thieves cannot get' " (Matt. 6:20, paraphrase).

Jesus said to him: "You know the commandments. Do not commit adultery. Do not kill. Do not steal. Do not bear false witness. Do not defraud. Honor your father and mother."

Naturally the young man replied as every good Jew would: "All these I have kept from my youth up." But Jesus already knew that. Was Jesus simply making sure that the young man saw the inadequacy of the Old Testament? The young man had kept the commandments perfectly and yet they were not satisfactory. The old way hadn't worked for him. "What must I do?"

Jesus stopped him there. "It is not that you must do something. You've done enough. You already have too many commandments to keep. I want to do something for you, son. My belief is not based on dos and don'ts. I'm a physician; you're my patient. I'm not your patient." "For whoever would save his life will lose it" (Matt. 16:25, RSV). "Quit trying so hard. The baby that struggles too hard has difficulty being born." "Jesus looking upon him loved him" (Mark 10:21, RSV). As Jesus watched this young man struggle against himself, his face torn between his "great possessions" and "a more excellent way," Jesus' heart went out to him. Hasn't this happened to you in some way? Some promising young man comes to you about his life. He doesn't know which way to turn. He addresses you with great respect. He is at the crossroads. What should he do?

I saw a banker's heart go out to such a young man. The youth told the banker he had been a gambler in a syndicate, and had been absolutely untrustworthy. Though his life had now changed, no one trusted him enough to establish him in a new business. He needed ten thousand dollars to start a bookstore. He didn't have any friends or references, not two nickles to rub together. And the banker, looking upon him, loved him and loaned him the money. I can just as easily see that banker looking upon him, loving him, and not loaning him the money, too.

Loving is so beautiful—taking a person to your heart. You see the tears. His yearning touches you and you would do anything for him. I see the young ruler affecting Jesus in a similar way. For a few seconds he was a complete stranger. Suddenly he was a brother, lost, outside in the darkness, knocking at the door. "Sir, tell me which way I should go?" The fact that he has more money, prestige, or formal education than Christ does not turn Jesus off. All these, which might be obstacles to us, were swept away. "Jesus loved him."

It is as if Jesus said:

I have a prescription for you. It is not for everyone. You lack one thing. Go sell all that you have and give it to the poor, and you will have treasure in heaven. Son, I want you to give up everything before it destroys you. It is all right for a man to own things, but not for things to own a man. You are not safe sitting on all those riches any more than an alcoholic is safe on a vat of wine. I want you to resign. I mean everything. Get rid of your office, your money, and all your land. Don't even pack a bag. Come along with me. The pressure on your heart will disappear. You'll be light as a feather. I could use another man. You'll make thirteen. I need a disciple with your experience. Most of my twelve are unschooled fishermen. You will help us reach the establishment. Come with me.

Did you ever hear a minister ask a man to give to God to save himself? Is that why people give? We tell each other to give to pay the preacher or to paint the buildings. Not Jesus. "Give before what you withheld gets you. You'll get lost if you haven't given."

This rich young ruler could have financed Jesus' evangelistic team for months. But Jesus didn't exploit that. Jesus told him to give to his favorite charity, as though he were asking him to dump contaminated material before it contaminated him. "I want you, not your estate. You matter to me. I don't care for what you make." That must have jarred the rich man. This is the reverse of most evangelists. They want what you have. Jesus never looked better: "Come. Leave everything behind. I'll show you where the treasure is. We must travel light to carry it."

The young man was torn by indecision. His life was at stake. How he longed to go with this young builder, fearless and free. People were standing around watching, but only the powerful man standing over him knew what he was going through. He had never undergone such agony before. The young man knew it was the turning point of his life. Was his eye concentrated then on a tiny

stone in front of his knee, on Jesus' sandal? He must stand
up and go one direction or the other. Perhaps he thought
of the banquet planned for him that night, the new
clothes he would wear, the chariot he had ordered, the
woman his family had planned for him to marry, the
house. This was too much.

Groaning, he got to his feet. Jesus helped him up,
looking deep into his tormented eyes. He could not do it.
"At these words his heart sank; for he was a very rich
man" (Luke 18:23, NEB). He had run to Jesus. Slowly he
walked away with Jesus' eyes on his back.

And Jesus looked around and said to his disciples,
" 'How hard it is for those who have riches to enter the
kingdom of God! For it is easier for a camel to go through
the eye of a needle than for a rich man to enter the kingdom of God.' Those who heard it said, 'Then who can be
saved?' But he said, 'What is impossible with men is
possible with God' " (Luke 18:24–27, RSV).

When Jesus says "rich man," he means us. To this
prophet who had only his robe and sandals, who had
nowhere to lay his head, and did not know where his next
meal was coming from, all of us who have food and a
warm place to sleep are fantastically rich. All Jesus' comments about the rich are aimed at us.

"It is easier for a camel to go through the eye of a
needle than for a rich man to enter the kingdom of God"
(Luke 18:25, RSV). "A fancy of the fifteenth century
suggested Jesus meant the 'needle's eye' gate, a small pos-
tern entrance beside the large city gate used after nightfall
and to be entered, it is argued, by a loaded camel upon its

knees . . . but such a gate was far too small for a camel loaded or unloaded; and whoever saw a camel crawl on its four knees!" (Interpreter's Bible, vol. 7, pp. 801, 807, exegesis). The Babylonian Talmud twice mentions the absurdity of an elephant going through the eye of a needle (Interpreter's Bible, vol. 7, p. 486). Jesus meant a needle. Mark used a Greek word referring to a housewife's needle. Luke used the Greek word for surgeon's needle. Jesus talked elsewhere of Pharisees straining gnats and swallowing camels. These are examples of Jesus' use of hyperbole; a camel simply cannot get through the eye of a needle.

"Then who can be saved?" (Mark 10:26, RSV). It is impossible except for God. A man can't make it on commandments. Getting people into heaven is God's work. If the rich young ruler couldn't make it, neither can we. Only God can do it. God created us. Only God can land a man on earth or in heaven.

The rich young ruler preferred to do it by himself. He refused Christ's help. He wanted some good hints for living, but he didn't want Christ to take over his life. He would have given Jesus one quarter of his holdings. Jesus held out his hand to the rich young ruler. It is so much easier to be good than to be God's. We can be good on our own, but in that there is no hope. Our hope is not based on our own goodness; it depends on Christ.

Peter began to say to Jesus,

"Lo, we have left everything and followed you. Lord, what are we going to get out of this? We've nothing left. We did what you told the rich young ruler to do." Jesus explained: "There is no one who has left house or brothers or sisters, mother or father, or children or lands for my sake or for the gospel who will not receive a hundredfold. Now in this time . . . and in the age to come eternal life" (Luke 18:28–30, paraphrase).

Before nightfall you will have a hundred times better than that tormented young man. You and I will possess the world. The sky is ours. We luxuriate in what the owner merely owns at great cost. The rich young ruler envies us. His world is on top of him. But we are on top of the world. Everything is reversed from the way it looks.

But many who are first will be last, and the last first (Matt. 19:30 NEB).

NOW when Jesus learned that the Pharisees had heard that he was making and baptising more disciples than John—although, in fact, it was not Jesus who did the baptising but his disciples—he left Judaea and went off again to Galilee, which meant his passing through Samaria. There he came to a Samaritan town called Sychar, which is near the plot of land that Jacob gave to his son, Joseph, and "Jacob's Spring" was there. Jesus tired with the journey, sat down beside it, just as he was. The time was about midday. Presently, a Samaritan woman arrived to draw some water.

"Please give me a drink," Jesus said to her, for his disciples had gone away to the town to buy food. The Samaritan woman said to him, "How can you, a Jew, ask for a drink from me, a woman of Samaria?" (For Jews have no dealings with Samaritans.)

"If you knew what God can give," Jesus replied, "and if you knew who it is that said to you, 'Give me a drink,' you would have asked him, and he would have given you living water!"

"Sir," said the woman, "you have no bucket and this well is deep—where can you get your living water? Are you a greater man than our ancestor, Jacob, who gave us this well, and drank here himself with his family, and his cattle?"

Jesus said to her, "Everyone who drinks this water will be thirsty again. But whoever drinks the water I will give him will never be thirsty again. For my gift will become a spring in the man himself, welling up into eternal life."

The woman said, "Sir, give me this water, so that I may stop being thirsty—and not have to make this journey to draw water any more!"

"Go and call your husband and then come back here," said Jesus to her.

"I haven't got a husband!" the woman answered.

"You are quite right in saying, 'I haven't got a husband,' " replied Jesus, "for you have had five husbands and the man you have now is not your husband at all. Yes, you spoke the truth when you said that."

"Sir," said the woman again, "I can see that you are a prophet! Now our ancestors worshipped on this hillside, but you Jews say that Jerusalem is the place where men ought to worship—"

"Believe me," returned Jesus, "the time is coming when worshipping the Father will not be a matter of 'on this hillside' or 'in Jerusalem.' Nowadays you are worshipping what you do not know. We Jews are worshipping what we know, for the salvation of mankind is to come from our race. Yet the time is coming, yes, and has already come, when true worshippers will worship the Father in spirit and in reality. Indeed, the Father looks for men who will worship him like that. God is Spirit, and those who worship him can only worship in spirit and in reality."

"Of course I know that Messiah is coming," returned the woman, "you know, the one who is called Christ. When he comes he will make everything plain to us."

"I am Christ speaking to you now," said Jesus.

At this point his disciples arrived, and were very surprised to find him talking to a woman, but none of them asked, "What do you want with her?" or "Why are you talking to her?" So the woman left her water-pot behind and went into the town and began to say to the people, "Come out and see the man who told me everything I've ever done! Can this be 'Christ'?" So they left the town and started to come to Jesus.

Meanwhile the disciples were begging him, "Master, do eat something."

To which Jesus replied, "I have food to eat that you know nothing about."

This, of course, made the disciples ask each other, "Do you think anyone has brought him any food?"

Jesus said to them, "My food is doing the will of him who sent me and finishing the work he has given me. Don't you say, 'Four months more and then comes the harvest'? But I tell you to open your eyes and look at the fields—they are gleaming white, all ready for the harvest! The reaper is already being rewarded and getting in a harvest for eternal life, so that both sower and reaper may be glad together. For in this harvest the old saying comes true, 'One man sows and another reaps.' I have sent you to reap a harvest for which you never laboured; other men have worked hard and you have reaped the result of their labours."

Many of the Samaritans who came out of that town believed in him through the woman's testimony—"He told me everything I've ever done." And when they arrived they begged him to stay with them. He did stay there two days and far more believed in him because of what he himself said. As they told the woman, "We don't believe any longer now because of what you said. We have heard him with our own ears. We know now that this really is the Saviour of the World!"

—JOHN 4:1–42, *Phillips*

6 / The Woman Who Had Five Husbands

Jesus' popularity created a crisis. His crowds swelled beyond those of John the Baptist and provoked the authorities. Since John had landed in prison and was finally beheaded for causing a disturbance, Jesus left Judea for home.

Jesus was not interested in whipping up the masses. He was after vows, not votes. Time after time he forsook the masses to face some individual. John's fourth chapter is another example.

To get home to Galilee from Judea, Jesus had to go through Samaria, the curse of Palestine to a Jew. Often Jews were killed while sneaking through Samaria. Bad blood had flowed between the two regions ever since the Samaritans had worshipped on the wrong mountain (Gerizim) instead of Jerusalem. A rabbi warned: "He that eats the bread of a Samaritan is like one who eats hog-flesh." Samaritans were for spitting on and spitting back. If Jews had to cross Samaria they would travel fast, avoiding all contact. However by noon on Jesus' trip through

Samaria he was hot and tired, so he decided to rest by Jacob's Well while his disciples took off for town to get food.

Jesus loved to be with people, but he also loved solitude. This is something each of the disciples had yet to learn for themselves, for when a trip was made to town everybody else went. It was no sacrifice to Christ to stay. Jesus knew how to make an exit as soon as he ran down. The Bible says he was exhausted. No doubt the disciples were too, but they couldn't sit still. They took off again. He stayed behind to save time in the long run.

Jesus' rest stop created this chapter in the Bible. However, his rest was interrupted, or was it? God arranged for someone to meet him: "A woman of Samaria came to draw water."

Jesus would have had every reason to expect to have that well all to himself at midday. Since women drew water evenings, any noon arrival would be exceptional. Jesus never regarded any interruption as routine. He would not even view it as an interruption. No one would come out there where Christ was resting except by an act of God.

To Jesus nothing was ever left to chance. The day may have been deadly hot, but with Jesus there the situation was portentous. Whoever walked over was walking into something. Should I say into a trap—or out of one? There was nothing but an old well, an odd woman, and a weary traveler. But that was enough.

Jesus just happened to stop for a breather at the same time a woman happened to go to the well. Perhaps the reason she was off schedule was because of her reputation. Had she gone at night when everyone else did she would have been stared down to the end of the line. It was all part of God's plan to save her town then and those reading about her now.

That woman would have expected Jesus to act as though she didn't exist. The most she could have expected from a Jew would have been a glare. She assumed she would appear obnoxious to him, for she was a Samaritan woman who had gone from bad to worse.

"Give me a drink" (John 4:7, RSV). For him to ask a favor of her was beyond belief. He was not sitting there in judgment upon her like everybody else. He approached her as a supplicant. That would have been overwhelming for any woman then. No decent man in those days would have spoken to a strange woman. Who would expect a Jew to contaminate his lips on a Samaritan's water jar? This man made himself vulnerable.

She is absolutely flabbergasted: "What! You a Jew asking a drink of me, a Samaritan woman?" It is surprising she found her voice to reply. But she is no mute drudge. Nor is she speechless with hate. She has rare spirit to speak up to a man in those days. This woman at Jacob's Well has Jacob's nerve. She showed courage to come alone. Would you have her courage to speak up like that to Him? She has the grace neither to ignore him, nor to solicit his attentions.

Had Jesus been waiting for someone special to come by? Did anyone who was not special ever come near him? Was he waiting for a drink? Waiting for God? Waiting for whoever God sent? He could wait. Here was the opening he always awaited, one which couldn't wait. She was thirstier than he.

Instead of being angry that she did not obey his request he gave up his drink to get one for her. "If you only knew what God gives, and who it is that is asking you for a drink, you would have asked him and he would have given you living water" (John 4:10, paraphase).

She had no doubt come to think that all there was to life was an everlasting round of heavy water jars. People forever thirsty, forever drinking and never quenching their thirst, endlessly, going nowhere until they drop. Jesus grasped her plight in a minute, her despair of this endless treadmill of trips and water jars. He was breaking through to her in her terms: "You don't know what water is."

" 'Sir,' said the woman, 'you have no bucket and this well is deep—where can you get your living water? Are you a greater man than our ancestor, Jacob, who gave us this well and drank here himself . . . ?' " (John 4:11–12, Phillips). Is she scornful? Is she saying: "You talk awfully big for someone without a bucket. Are you too good for this well? It was good enough for Jacob." Most evangelists would have lost their temper or lost heart by this time, and thought, "the kingdom will come before this woman ever sees the light." But the well Jesus proposed is a deep subject.

Jesus persisted. "Everyone who drinks this water will be thirsty again, but whoever drinks the water that I will give him will never be thirsty again" (John 4:14, Phillips). "No matter how much you drink of this water, you'll have to do it all over again soon, but if you'll drink what I can give you it will prime your own interior spring that won't run dry. Drink this and you'll drink the well."

What will she think? Was this strange man suffering from the heat? But she had been suffering from the same heat all her life. Was he being ridiculous? Yet what could be more ridiculous than the way her life was, the object of ridicule, and with her water jar still empty after all the trips she had made? He had turned her water off.

She was about ready for another life. Was there a better life? There was something artesian about him. Could she tap his inner resources? Was she hallucinating, or was this hope? She replied, perhaps tartly, perhaps wistfully, "Sir, give me this water, so that I may stop being thirsty—and not have to make this journey to draw water any more!" (John 4:15, Phillips).

Then Jesus plunged into her heart: "Go, call your husband and come here" (John 4:16, RSV). The water Jesus had to give was not mere surface sprinkling. She needed this water where she was rooted, where she was attached. The water Jesus was concerned with had to do with the way she lived her life. She retorted lamely: "I have no husband." This time she would not get away with that. Suddenly her past caught up with her: "You are quite right," said Jesus, "for you have had five husbands and he whom you now have is not your husband." (John 4:18, RSV). Jesus' water was no longer a wild idea. He had poured the cup for her to drink. It was hard, and clear.

Discovering this woman's past did not diminish Jesus' good will toward her. Nothing she could have done would have turned him off. He was not there to criticize her, but to bring her refreshment. He didn't ridicule her alibi, but he did not want it to stand between them. If the woman is astounded by his knowing all about her, she must be literally undone by his tenderness when he knows the worst.

Is she trembling as she tries to dodge him? "Sir," she replies, "I see that you are a prophet. Our fathers worshipped on this mountain, but you Jews say that the temple where God should be worshipped is in Jerusalem." Hasn't everyone tried that? Someone suggests prayer, and we stall with, "Let's talk *about* prayer." When God becomes too close we put him off into a discussion.

So when Jesus starts to untangle her from the stranglehold of six men, she hides behind this tired argument over which place to have church. Jesus' incisions are close to where she hurts. Isn't that the way with us? We all prefer to shoot the breeze rather than to have surgery.

Jesus won't let her get away. His answer draws her to the verge of life. "Believe me," returned Jesus, "the time is coming when worshipping the Father will not be a matter of 'on this hill-side' or 'in Jerusalem' " (John 4:21, Phillips). She has been in a panic to get the conversation safely on to Jerusalem, but Jesus suggests, "My dear, right here will do very nicely for you to meet God."

She makes one final frantic attempt to escape: "I know that Christ is coming. When he comes he will tell us everything." Since Jesus won't let the conversation wander to Jerusalem, she agrees that her meeting with God could be by this well, but she postpones it to some time in the future. She heaves a sigh of relief and says, "Not until Christ comes." Then Jesus announces: "I am he." She is his.

Just then his disciples return from town, no doubt shocked to find him alone with this woman. They make a point of not saying anything about it. The woman flees without her water jar. Where do you suppose she went? Far as she could go from that well? Into hiding? To all five husbands? Where would you have gone? Would you have told anyone?

This woman took off for town to tell everybody. In the Bible, she says: "Come see a man who told me all that I ever did. Can this be Christ?" Such a comment from such a woman must have made many people in town nervous. In any event, one woman with conviction had the effect of a fire. John says that the people poured out of the city and headed toward Jacob's Well.

Meanwhile back at the well the disciples were unable to get Jesus to eat their food. He insisted he had eaten while they were gone, from provisions they didn't know he had. "So the disciples said to one another, "His anyone brought him food?" (John 4:33, RSV).

Jesus had just delivered life to a woman with a drink of water; now he was attempting it for his disciples with the meat they brought. "My food is doing the will of Him who sent me and finishing the work he has given me" (John 4:34, Phillips). In other words:

Lunch isn't satisfying, for one soon wants supper. We can stuff ourselves, but it won't stifle the craving long. We have an appetite that isn't touched by feasting. For instance, if I had drunk that woman's well water, by this time I would be ready for another drink. But God wanted me to lead her into deep water, and doing His will filled me up. I want you all to share this satisfaction. You can't imagine what a banquet I attended in your absence. Doing this little thing for God has made me all over new again. How many overstuffed lives are starving for this finer food? Look around the fields; they are already white, ripe for harvest. God used others to plant. I want you to harvest. Look, there is a whole town starved for this bread.

The townspeople begged Jesus to stay, simply on the word of this disreputable woman. What a preacher she was, or was it merely her change that overwhelmed them?

The disciples went to town, and all they got out of it was groceries. Jesus waited by the well, but the town came to him. "He stayed there two days" (John 4:40, RSV). Christianity cannot be experienced secondhand. The woman brought the town to Christ. "It is no longer because of your words that we believe, for we have heard for ourselves" (John 4:42, RSV). "Many more believed because of his word" (John 4:41, RSV).

Jesus himself is waiting for you the next time you get up to have a drink. Will you give him a drink if he asks you? Will you let him give *you* a drink? He won't mention five husbands to you, but he will relate to your inmost being. Will you put it off? Now? Here? The time is ripe. Come. The ripeness won't last forever.

THEN he went into Jericho and was making his way through it. And here we find a wealthy man called Zacchaeus, a chief collector of taxes, wanting to see what sort of person Jesus was. But the crowd prevented him from doing so, for he was very short. So he ran ahead and climbed up into a sycamore tree to get a view of Jesus as he was heading that way. When Jesus reached the spot, he looked up and said to him,

"Zacchaeus, hurry up and come down. I must be your guest today."

So Zacchaeus hurriedly climbed down and gladly welcomed him. But the bystanders muttered their disapproval, saying,

"Now he has gone to stay with a real sinner."

But Zacchaeus himself stood and said to the Lord,

"Look, sir, I will give half my property to the poor. And if I have swindled anybody out of anything I will pay him back four times as much."

Jesus said to him,

"Salvation has come to this house today! Zacchaeus is a descendant of Abraham, and it was the lost that the Son of Man came to seek—and to save."

—LUKE 19:1–10, *Phillips*

7 / A Hated Man

The road from Jerusalem to Jericho was so rough with armed robbery that we still remember Jesus' story of one of the crimes. But Jericho was worth the risk. It was a showplace surrounded by prosperous groves of palms and balsam. Mark Anthony thought Jericho was a gem and gave it to Cleopatra. Death found Herod there. No wonder cutthroats liked to wait behind the rocks a little way out of town and work over anyone entering or leaving the Bank of Jericho.

Even more crooks stayed in town, fleecing the natives with the government's backing. They were the tax collectors, and Jericho was a plum for them. It took a bustling hive of agents to pick it clean. "And there was a man named Zacchaeus; he was a chief tax collector, and rich" (Luke 19:2, RSV).

The word tax collector was a swearword, not a compliment. Everybody hates taxes, but in those days the only people who had to pay taxes were the conquered. Taxes infuriated the Jews because it reminded them they were chained to Caesar. The money did not stay in Jerusalem but went to Rome.

Worse yet, Rome paid Jews to do this dirty work. Any Jew who would do that would rob, and tax collectors were well known for this. The collectors' huge rake-off created as much of a scandal as the crates shipped out of the country. Whoever Zacchaeus was, he was in the dirtiest business in town. Wherever he went he would be hissed. No one would want to be seen with him. He and his children would not receive any invitations to dinner. At the first sign of a riot, he would be the first to leave. He was well advised to avoid large crowds and dark alleys.

"He was trying to see who Jesus was." Zacchaeus was not after Jesus' autograph. Jesus had just opened the eyes of a blind man. But what could Jesus do for Zacchaeus? Zaccheus isn't poor and he isn't sick; Zaccheus had been condemned.

Jesus was said to prefer tax collectors to church officials. He even ate with them. He made one of them (Matthew) his secretary, according to E. J. Goodspeed. Who could guess how much it would mean to Zacchaeus to have a place to go and not have to force his way in—to be expected somewhere? Would Jesus actually have time for a man like him? What would it be like for Zacchaeus to meet a man who would pay attention to him instead of taxes? That town was filled with people whose homes were not open to Zacchaeus. There would be no mourning for him when he died, and if he fell, laughter.

But how could Zacchaeus ever see Jesus? Hostile faces tried to keep bad elements like Zacchaeus away from Jesus. Zacchaeus tried desperately to squeeze into the center of the crowd. It might have been difficult for a big man, "but he was a little man" (Luke 19:3, TEV), not to mention his demeaning job. "Oh, no you don't." Zacchaeus, however, was determined to reach Jesus at any cost. He noticed that the procession was headed toward the southern gate, and he saw a sycamore tree standing in Jesus' path. "So he ran ahead of the crowd and climbed . . ." (Luke 19:4, TEV).

Did you ever lie in wait for Christ? Did you ever go to church where he was expected, ahead of everybody else? We stare at a hole in our suit: "I can't go to church in *that*." We look out the window at the storm: "We can't go out in *this*." How many would stay home if there was standing room only? How many of us walk to church but wouldn't run to beat the crowd? Would we go if the only room left was up in a tree? Zacchaeus wanted to see Jesus so badly he sprinted to a sycamore, shinnied up, and went out on a limb to lie in wait.

When Jesus came to that place he looked up and said, "Zacchaeus, make haste and come down; for I must stay at your house today" (Luke 19:5, RSV). For once someone had called him Zacchaeus. Jesus knew his name. He had gone to the trouble of learning it. Jesus acted as though he had made the long trip to Jericho just to look up Zacchaeus. Zacchaeus had yearned for years to have someone to dinner. Was Jesus his first guest? The Sabbath was about to begin and Jesus declared he would spend it with Zacchaeus. Jesus would likely be asked to speak at the synagogue. The guest speaker would be staying at the house of Zacchaeus. It was the last Sabbath of Christ's life. "Zacchaeus, I would like to spend my last Sabbath with you."

Zaccheus could not believe his ears. The sound of that voice shook him out of the tree. After a lifetime of people avoiding him, someone wanted him. "Zacchaeus hurried down and welcomed him with great joy" (Luke 19:6, TEV).

The crowd was horrified. Jesus was going to stay at the house of public enemy number one. Imagine that! Jesus visits our beautiful city, knowing that he can stay wherever he likes, and he chooses to spend the night in Watergate. Jesus lost his crowd right there. This was a blow, which infuriated everybody. People were groveling at Christ's feet in a frenzy to crown him, until they discovered Jesus loved tax collectors. Well, they would see about that on Friday.

Jericho had damned Zacchaeus for years. He was their scapegoat, the one they blamed for everything that went wrong. The reason why the world was in this mess was because of tax collectors. No one other than Christ had ever said a prayer for Zacchaeus. Zacchaeus was sent threatening notes, and his yard was full of rocks.

Christ would not join the crowd. You never know what they will throw next—thrones or rocks. Jesus didn't appreciate crowds; he preferred one man at a time. The mob would get him in a few days, but that would not distract him from saving one more man. A man's drawbacks never fooled Jesus; he saw the man. Zacchaeus was guilty, but Jesus did not come to press charges. There's a bad side to the best man, and the worst man could be even worse. But the fact a man has cheated does not make him a cheater to the end. He saw past an individual's problems to the emerging man. He saw Zacchaeus as God meant him to be. Men are not dead wrong; they are only wrong.

Zacchaeus had possibly accepted that tax job with reservations. Perhaps his older brother had inherited everything. Perhaps his wife wouldn't agree to marry him unless he could come up with material goods. But it agonized him to be thrown in with the Romans. His employers treated him like dirt. Every day that he walked into the tax building it twisted a knife in his heart. Zacchaeus was not an unfeeling post. His way of life was affecting him.

Had Jesus seen the little man making the end run at the edge of the crowd? Jesus was always singling someone out. He didn't miss much. When Jesus reached the tree, he stopped the procession to study the face above his head—a face working with emotion. Zacchaeus was hoping against all hope that someone would recognize his face and see there was a man behind it waiting his turn, a man who would do anything to redeem himself, but who was stuck in a tree. Jesus saw a man whose face had had doors slammed in it for years, and his heart went out to that man all alone up there, out in the cold.

Jesus made a big decision. He decided to side with Zacchaeus against the crowd. He knew what it would cost. He would lose more than an audience, but he would draw the fire away from Zacchaeus. That was like Christ. Time after time Jesus could have had the nation. Wasn't he King David's son? "Did you hear that crowd yelling out there?"

"No, thank you, I'll take the man in the tree."

"Hurry down, Zacchaeus, for I must stay at your house today." Zacchaeus perceived in a moment the high price that Christ had just paid with those brave words. Christ had ignored the town, and now had the entire town on his neck for the sake of Zacchaeus. Jesus had tossed his reputation up into a tree in exchange for Zacchaeus.

"All the people who saw it started grumbling. This man has gone as a guest to the house of a sinner" (Luke 19:7, TEV). They said, "This man," no longer calling him "Rabbi."

It was time for the real Zacchaeus to stand up for the first man to ever stand up for him. All that Jesus spent there on Zacchaeus prepared Zacchaeus to make a statement that caused the walls of Jericho to tumble down again. Such momentous words from this little man have caused us to be affected by them after twenty centuries. Christ did his part; then Zacchaeus came through. "Listen, sir, I will give half my belongings to the poor; And if I have cheated anyone I will pay him back four times as much" (Luke 19:8, TEV).

That is quite a pledge from an unpromising prospect. We always think about how much good our pledge will do for others. But what good will it do the donor? That pledge saved the donor's life. "Jesus said to him, 'Today salvation has come to this house . . . for the Son of man came to seek and to save the lost' " (Luke 19:9–10, RSV).

Who are *we* to talk about somebody up a tree? What goes up must come down. Anyone high and dry today is a candidate for this specialist of the lost. Perhaps some of us are lost in the crowd, but others of us are stranded on some limb. Perhaps Christianity's not really a climb, but merely requires getting down safely from our tree. Look down from your perch. Someone may be looking up at you, ready to take you to dinner. Come on down and live.

ONE night Nicodemus, a leading Jew and a Pharisee, came to see Jesus.

"Rabbi," he began, "we realize that you are a teacher who has come from God. For no one could show the signs that you show unless God were with him."

"Believe me," returned Jesus, "when I assure you that a man cannot see the kingdom of God without being born again."

"And how can a man who has grown old possibly be born?" replied Nicodemus. "Surely he cannot go into his mother's womb a second time to be born?"

"I do assure you," said Jesus, "that unless a man is born from water and from spirit he cannot enter the kingdom of God. Flesh gives birth to flesh and spirit gives birth to spirit: you must not be surprised that I told you that all of you must be born again. The wind blows where it likes, you can hear the sound of it but you have no idea where it comes from or where it goes. Nor can you tell how a man is born by the wind of the Spirit."

"How on earth can things like this happen?" replied Nicodemus.

"So you are the teacher of Israel," said Jesus, "and you do not understand such things? I assure you that we are talking about what we know and we are witnessing to what we have observed, yet you will not accept our evidence. Yet if I have spoken to you about things which happen on this earth and you will not believe me, what chance is there that you will believe me if I tell you about what happens in Heaven? No one has ever been up to Heaven except the Son of Man who came down from Heaven. The Son of Man must be lifted above the heads of men—as Moses lifted up that serpent in the desert—so that any man who believes in him may have eternal life. For God loved the world so much that he gave his only Son, so that everyone who believes in him should not be lost, but should have eternal life. God has not sent his Son into the world to pass sentence upon it, but to save it— through him. Any man who believes in him is not judged at all. It is the one who will not believe who stands already condemned, because he will not believe in the character of God's only Son. This *is* the judgment—that light has entered the world and men have preferred darkness to light because their deeds were evil. Everybody who does wrong hates the light and keeps away from it, for fear his deeds may be exposed. But everybody who is living by the truth will come to the light to make it plain that all he has done has been done through God."

—JOHN 3:1–21, *Phillips*

8 / A Powerful Politician

The day you take your first breath is a big day. That's life. That's your day. You'll celebrate that day until you die. Nothing that could possibly happen to us could ever equal our birth unless it is repeated.

This brings us to the third chapter of John. A man in a high public office looked up Jesus one night and they had a talk about birth.

Too much has been made of Nicodemus's not having the nerve to contact Christ in broad daylight. Of course, no man cares to have it widely known that he can't find the answer himself. No one likes to have everybody see another person help him to his feet. But that is not why Nicodemus came late at night.

The wonder is not that Nicodemus came by night, but that he came at all. Nicodemus probably could not have paid that call by day and lived to tell about it. Jesus had just cleaned out the temple in the previous paragraph. He put some pretty important people—Pharisees—out of business there, and into the business of killing him. Nicodemus was one of their chief officers. Jesus had en-

joyed a bad name with the people in power for a long
time. He had barely escaped stoning several times. The
night Nicodemus met Christ, the final plan for Christ's
execution was afoot. Anyone seen with him would be
suspect. Nicodemus ran quite a risk that night.

What brought Nicodemus out on a night like that? He
opened the conversation. "We know, Rabbi, that you are
a teacher sent by God. No one could do the mighty works
you are doing unless God were with him." Nicodemus
addresses Christ with great respect.

Jesus won't let him get away with that. Nicodemus
didn't risk coming just to pay Jesus a compliment. Jesus
is brutal because he wants to break Nicodemus's pride.
Jesus was not facing a poor beaten victim of life this time.
Nicodemus was part of the power structure hunting him
down and planning to do him in. Nicodemus needed to
be sprung. Jesus went after him. "No one can *see* the
kingdom of God unless he is born again" (John 3:3, TEV).

"Nicodemus, you have stumbled out here tonight for
nothing if all I can do is teach and doctor. You need to be
reconceived. Paying your respects to me is deadly. There
is nothing to discuss. I want you to go through the door.
You don't need any more lessons or more religious activi-
ties. It is high time for you to change."

Nicodemus does not understand. "How can a man
who has grown old possibly be born? "Certainly he cannot enter his mother's womb and be born a second time"
(Good News, John 3:4).

"Wait a minute, Jesus. You impress me. I have risked
everything to follow you here tonight but you've lost me.

Becoming a good person is like climbing. Practice makes perfect. God doesn't lift you; you have to use your elbows and legs. No one gave me my seat. I took it."

"Nicodemus, whatever you can do for yourself won't be enough." "I tell you the truth," replied Jesus, "that *no one* can enter the kingdom of God unless he is born of water and the spirit" (John 3:5, TEV). As if to say:

> You must find another mother. You will die of stillbirth if you won't come out of the womb where you are. Another umbilical cord must be cut, new eyes opened, ears that hear better. Your first birth brought you to earth; this new birth bears you into the kingdom you can't strain your way into. Worry and work won't add an inch to your growth. And the heights you attain in my kingdom come the same way you got your first eyes and ears and hands and feet. You don't push your way into love, you fall in, and it is like being on another planet. You are transported to another style of life.

"Flesh gives birth to flesh and spirit gives birth to spirit . . ." (John 3:6, Phillips).

This is easier to believe about someone who has gone to hell and then come back. An alcoholic priest told me he was so far gone that he fortified his pockets and strapped flat flasks to his legs under his trousers before he left the house in the morning. One morning, bulging with bottles, he fell off the front steps, felt something wet running down his leg and found himself saying, "Please God, let it be blood."

Obviously that fellow was beyond the reach of mere

talking. Drying him out would only get him ready for the next spree. No psychiatrist would give him encouragement. You couldn't shame him out of it. More resolutions only made it more ridiculous. He had already promised himself several times a day for years that he would stop. He will promise anything. "I'll never touch another drop." But it is all talk, until that day he reaches out and cries "Help!" and God grabs him hard and mothers him again. Then he may be able to burst out of the world he was in and into life.

Many alcoholics have not only been sober for years, they have become different men and women. All alcoholics would agree that they became sober not by trying, but by giving up.

God didn't do a job simply on the addiction but on a complete change of heart. The most noticeable thing is not that an alcoholic has stopped drinking, but that he has started over again on the ground floor with everybody else.

Granted that something radical is required to resurrect a dead drunk, but surely not Nicodemus. On the contrary, Jesus is holding this momentous conversation on radical personal change, not with a deadbeat but with a bishop of the Jewish church. The name Nicodemus means "victor of the people." Jesus is taking this high church official apart, and telling him he has to be put back together again in a different way. Nicodemus gave much of himself to God; he was a religious expert. Jesus was speaking to a man whose mother was proud of him. And Jesus was telling this man who had turned out so well that he was good for nothing unless he began all over again.

Nicodemus, God's not interested in your obituary. Your charities are just pretty stepping stones. Your reputation is paper, your life is a museum piece, a front. You are living in a tomb of religious exercises. You are duty bound with dos and don'ts. Where is it getting you? What are you getting out of it? Why are you doing it? You are not free. You don't love. You Pharisees worry how you look.

"You clean the outside of the cup and the dish, while the inside is full of greed and self-indulgence" (Matt. 23:25, Phillips). "You are death to anybody who disagrees with you." "You scour sea and land to make a single convert, and then you make him twice as ripe for destruction as you are yourselves" (Matt. 23:15, Phillips).

What have you got for all this religious activity, Nicodemus? It doesn't make anybody happy. Nicodemus, your religion is too cut and dry. I came to save people from the religious freight you carry. Who would want a life like yours? I came to take you away from all this. Nicodemus, you carry God in your pocket. But I want to carry you in God's pocket. Your church attendance is a grind. Let me comfort you. Nicodemus, you've made religion torture, but it is a birthday. God wants you to celebrate. You've made work for yourself. You'll worship not because you had better, but because you can't stop. Let me deliver you. Nicodemus, hold still, let go, let me send you.

"Do not marvel that I said to you, 'You must be born anew.' The wind blows where it wills, and you hear the sound of it, but you do not know whence it comes or whither it goes; so it is with every one who is born of the Spirit. . . . Are you a teacher of Israel, and yet you do not understand this?" (John 3:7–8, 10, RSV).

"I cannot explain it, Nicodemus, except to say that you don't need moral improvement; you are conscientious enough. You need to give up and yield to God."

"And as Moses lifted up the serpent in the wilderness, so must the Son of man be lifted up . . ." (John 3:14, RSV). In the wilderness when the Israelites went through a place infested with poisonous snakes, God had Moses erect a brass serpent. If anyone was bitten he was to look at the brass serpent and be saved. All of us have been bitten, either by weakness or by strength. Failure can bite, as well as success. Life infects us unless we look up to Him and reflect on Him. Our only hope is in Christ.

Our snakebite may not seem fatal at first. It may not look as bad as that of the prostitute; it may not swell as quickly as the drunkard's. But the devil is here. Man has fallen. Not even Nicodemus escaped. All have been bitten. "And as Moses lifted up the serpent in the wilderness" (and men were saved by looking upon it) "so must the Son of Man be lifted up" (John 3:14, RSV). He was lifted up on the cross and so we shed our skin as we keep looking upon his face. "For God so loved the world that he gave his only son, that whoever believes in him should not perish but have eternal life" (John 3:16, RSV).

Things happened fast after that night. Once when the chief priests and Pharisees were seeking to arrest Christ, it was Nicodemus who stood up to them all, risking everything to say: "Does our law judge a man without first giving him a hearing . . . ?" (John 7:51, RSV).

After Christ was crucified and everyone had washed their hands of Him, the disciples fled, and the Marys would not return for another day and two nights. But on that same night, Good Friday, a man went to the cross while Christ was still warm. Like the kings who had brought myrrh to the barn beneath the star, he carried a hundred pounds of myrrh. It was Nicodemus. In order to risk this trip, Nicodemus broke the Sabbath, which began at sundown. He would have had trouble finding a porter. Did Nicodemus carry one hundred pounds himself? He was the only one mentioned who helped Joseph of Arimathea let Christ down from the cross and into the grave in the garden.

That was a night spent with Christ. Have you seen Rembrandt's painting of Joseph and Nicodemus on their scaffolding, lowering Christ from the cross; or Michelangelo's sculpture of Nicodemus tenderly holding the body of Christ in his arms, with the carved face of Nicodemus resembling that of Michelangelo? It must have been Nicodemus's birthday. Nothing less could have brought him out there again that perilous night to fight upstream against a mob stampeding in the other direction. Something was going on in Nicodemus of such mammoth proportions that it could only be described by the words: "If any man be in Christ, he is a new creature . . ." (2 Cor. 5:17, KJV).

EARLY next morning he returned to the Temple and the entire crowd came to him. So he sat down and began to teach them. But the scribes and Pharisees brought in to him a woman who had been caught in adultery. They made her stand in front, and then said to him, "Now, master, this woman has been caught in adultery, in the very act. According to the Law, Moses commanded us to stone such women to death. Now, what do you say about it?"

They said this to test him, so that they might have some good grounds for an accusation. But Jesus stooped down and began to write with his finger in the dust on the ground. But as they persisted in their questioning, he straightened himself up and said to them, "Let the one among you who has never sinned throw the first stone at her." Then he stooped down again and continued writing with his finger on the ground. And when they heard what he said, they were convicted by their own consciences and went out, one by one, beginning with the eldest.

Jesus was left alone, with the woman still standing where they had put her. So he stood up and said to her, "Where are they all—did no one condemn you?"

And she said, "No one, sir."

"Neither do I condemn you," said Jesus to her. "Go away now and do not sin again."

—JOHN 8:1–11, *Phillips*

9 / The Woman Caught

"The teachers of the law and the Pharisees brought in a woman who had been caught committing adultery, and made her stand before them all. 'Teacher,' they said to Jesus, 'this woman was caught in the very act. . . . Moses gave a commandment that such a woman must be stoned to death. Now what do you say?' They said this to trap Him" (John 8:3–6, Good News for Modern Man).

This woman's life was not the only one in danger at that moment. So was Christ's. Both their lives were hanging on his answer. He would have to condemn her or be condemned for breaking the law.

People from all over Palestine had been packing the temple all week to hear Christ. But his sermons were splitting the crowds for and against him. John's previous chapter is torn with the controversy. "Does he have a demon in him or is this actually Christ? How does he know so much? He never went to school. Is he any good or is he an imposter?" To one side he was God, to the other no better than a dog. The poor worshipped the ground on which he walked, the Pharisees cursed it. Several times they had their hands on the very stones to beat him to death, but while they were taking aim he disappeared.

The day before they had dispatched guards to arrest him, but a ruler of the Jews named Nicodemus stood in their way. Now since sentiment was almost evenly divided, perhaps a carefully staged incident could swing the sympathy against him. Violence had failed, so now they would frame him. That is why they dragged this woman into the picture. Perhaps she was raped, or they may have paid someone to get her into trouble. I doubt if they questioned her closely. They omitted mentioning the man. They were using her to bait the hook for Him.

They flung her in front of everybody to wait for the signal. She was finished either way. The law required that an unfaithful wife should be strangled. Stoning was reserved for incidents involving a betrothed damsel or a priest's daughter. If a woman were both, she was to be burned. Was she praying for them to get it over with? Was she witnessing her last judgment? Did she wonder who He was? He was on trial for his life too. Was it the first time someone had shared her predicament?

"Jesus bent down and wrote on the ground with his finger" (John 8:6, Good News for Modern Man). Was he stalling for time? They kept harping at him, "Come on, yes or no." Jesus would not be rushed. He took his time even though he had only a few minutes left. You could not pressure him. He could not be threatened. The devil had tried. Jesus was writing in the sand. Why should he allow the Pharisees to stampede him? They were not

Gods. He wrote "as though he heard them not" (John 8:6 KJV). This was only a mob, and he was concentrating on something else. What did he write? Kahlil Gibran said that Christ wrote down the names of every man and beside each name the man's sin. Whatever he did with the sand, the effect on the people was devastating. They came to see to him, but he saw through them. They selected another's sin, but he found them steeped in sin. While they were trying to pin something on her, he exposed them. They had planned for her case to come up; instead it was theirs. Judgment day came down upon them all. They had set a trap for him. But he caught them in it.

They kept pushing closer to him. He had kept them at bay while he was stooped down writing. "He straightened up" (John 8:7, TEV). Did he tower over them? When Christ straightened up how tall would he be? What emptied the courtroom that day? Was it his height? He silenced them by standing. Then he let them have it: " 'Let him who is without sin among you be the first to throw a stone at her.' And once more he bent down and wrote with his finger on the ground" (John 8:7–8, RSV).

They squirmed like schoolboys before this man. He dismissed that lynch mob with a look. Jesus did not make a mass arrest. He identified each man: guilty. They took off one by one, "beginning with the eldest" (John 8:9, KJV), which is the reverse of the way they voted in the Sanhedrin. Did he have more on the older men? They came to murder him. He demolished every single one.

"Jesus was left alone, with the woman still standing where they had put her" (John 8:9, Phillips). This will happen to each of us in the end. We'll be alone with Christ. He will know more than we know about ourselves. It will be a hard day for those who think it will be easy. "For nothing is . . . hidden that shall not be made known" (Matt. 10:26, KJV). We shall finally see that we are helpless without his intervention.

Of course our trial will be fair, but if it is only fair we are doomed. Remember Shakespeare's words in *The Merchant of Venice:* "For if justice be our plea, why none should see salvation." It all depends, as it did for that woman, whether someone will shield us from the stones we deserve and grant us mercy. There was only one man who survived on his performance; the rest of us will never make it without his help.

The woman was now far more frightened of him than by the multitude. She could get lost in the crowd. One is amazed she did not flee from him. She would have had to face those eyes; the trial before the crowd was nothing compared to that. They were as bad as she was. He was not. Their eyes were cold. His burned into the soul. "Who can endure the day of His coming, and who can stand when He appears?" (Mal. 3:2, RSV).

He had come to her, and his eyes weighed heavier on her than stones. In them she could see herself as she really was. It was not a pretty sight. If only he would accuse her it would make it so much easier. Those others had no right; only He had the right. He had just saved her life. He kept writing in the sand. She was done for now.

Mercy does not mean we get off lightly. That woman could have died a thousand deaths more easily than stand before the judgment seat of Christ. Mercy will break your heart. It doesn't mean justice wasn't done. It was more than done. It was that he took the blame for her. He takes the punishment we deserve. Someday we'll see that we haven't paid all our debts. Someday we'll see, and we'll never be the same. That woman was seeing. She was not impudent. She did not speak out loud. Inside Christ might have heard her say, "Oh speak, please speak. I cannot go on living unless you speak—to me."

"He straightened up and said to her, 'Where are they? Is there no one left to condemn you?'

'No one, sir,' she answered" (John 8:10, TEV). The verdict that mattered to her was not yet in. She could have run off as soon as her accusers left, but she remained standing, waiting for him. Another woman would have fled from the place of her humiliation on the instant of release. "I'll be more careful after this." He gave her the right to go. He would not have to know; he was bent down writing in the sand. She chose to stay for the hardest part. No matter how much it hurt, she wanted his opinion. He had returned her life to her, but she would not accept it without him.

Jesus knew that something had happened to hold that woman there while he was looking the other way. That was her way of thanking him. He had captured her full attention. Would he throw her back into the same pond from which she had been taken? Was she unredeemable in his eyes? Was he only going to return her to her old life? Had he saved her on a whim, or was it possible he had something else in his mind for her? She could not bear to go back, but was she good for anything else? The question this horrid day had wrung from her was simply: Is there anything else? Had he washed his hands of her? Had he forgotten she was waiting for his answer?

He looked up; at last he was sentencing her. She must have been numb with fear and shame and hope, when he said, "Neither do I condemn thee: go, and sin no more" (John 8:11, KJV). Did she hear right? Could it be true that he had not only saved her but had absolved her, that the way was clear for her to walk away free at last? Suddenly the writing in the sand made sense to her. The form of the word *woman* he used for her meant *lady*. "You have been saved not only from death but from hell itself."

AFTER Jesus had said this, he was clearly in anguish of soul, and he added, solemnly

"I tell you plainly, one of you is going to betray me."

At this the disciples stared at each other, completely mystified as to whom he could mean. And it happened that one of them, whom Jesus loved, was sitting very close to him. So Simon Peter nodded to this man and said, "Tell us who he means."

He simply leaned forward on Jesus' shoulder, and asked, "Lord, who is it?"

And Jesus answered, "It is the one I am going to give this piece of bread to, after I have dipped it in the dish."

Then he took a piece of bread, dipped it in the dish and gave it to Simon's son, Judas Iscariot. After he had taken the piece of bread, Satan entered his heart. Then Jesus said to him, "Be quick about your business!"

No one else at the table knew what he meant in telling him this. Indeed, some of them thought that, since Judas had charge of the purse, Jesus was telling him to buy what they needed for the festival, or that he should give something to the poor. So Judas took the piece of bread and went out quickly—into the night.

When he had gone, Jesus spoke, "Now comes the glory of the Son of Man, and the glory of God in him! If God is glorified through him then God will glorify the Son of Man —and that without delay."

—JOHN 13:21–31, *Phillips*

10 / His Traitor

"And Judas Iscariot" is at the bottom of the lists of disciples in the New Testament. Some say *Iscariot* means "man from Kerioth," a city in the south of Judea. Others say it comes from the Aramaic, meaning the false assassin, although Judas is described as the son of Simon Iscariot. While there was a good Judas too among the twelve, and mixed feelings about the betrayer, no one has since wanted to name a child or even a dog Judas.

However, we cannot talk about Judas as though he is one of "them" and therefore not like "us." In this awful thing that happened to Christ we approach Judas not as the innocent one but as his accomplice. The betrayal of Christ cannot be placed on Judas alone. It is something that involves anyone who is human.

Judas's act terrifies us because he did boldly what we try to get away with on the sly. Have you never turned on Christ or sold out on him? Have you never turned him in? Have you never made money on Christ? Am I writing this book about Jesus to make a profit on him? Isn't your church affiliation good for business? Won't church be to your children's advantage?

Judas is no different from us except in his candor. What makes us think our own rooting around the cross is so superior? Are we looking to Jesus for his sake or ours? We must see how terribly implicated we are in his arrest. "Were you there when they crucified my Lord?" Do you answer, "Sometimes it causes me to tremble"? Even the disciples bravely asked Jesus: "Lord, is it I?" Have you ever asked Jesus that? It says in the Gospels that "All the disciples forsook him and fled" (Matt. 26:56; Mark 14:50, RSV). And the rooster crowed for the very one who vowed he'd never forsake Christ. Have we been more faithful than the twelve?

In Rembrandt's 1633 painting, *The Raising of the Cross,* for Prince Frederick Henry of Orange, a man in a painter's beret raises Christ upon the cross. That is a self-portrait of Rembrandt himself [Francis Schaeffer, *How Then Shall We Live* (Old Tappan, New Jersey: Fleming H. Revell Co., 1976), p. 98].

Haven't you ever wanted Jesus out of the way? Judas is a hard subject to master. There are mirrors all about. No one who knows the black depths of his own heart will treat Judas as simply another villain. What about the times I have kissed Christ? Have I had him arrested too? Was I so faithful to Christ when he was profaned at my last party? This chapter may turn out to be our confession.

How could Jesus ever have had a disciple like Judas? Apparently, Jesus made Judas treasurer of the disciples. Was Jesus mistaken about this man? Was Jesus compelled not only to carry his cross, but to pick the man who would fix him on it? Somehow Jesus had to die for us. And we

did it to him through Judas, Peter, Pilate, and the wretch-
edness that gets hold of a crowd like that.

The crime of Judas was not by chance. The devil had
fouled God's good creation. God sent his Son to straighten
it out. Then the devil got Judas and Caiaphas to collabo-
rate on a cross, but that all played into God's hand. Can
you imagine anything worse than the cross? What is more
damnable than to kill Him like that? Where was there
ever more innocent blood, more savage guilt? And yet
what happened at that intersection of good and evil has
become the old, old story that has taught us to sing: "In
the cross of Christ I glory."

Though Jesus was not manipulated by the devil nor
programmed as the pawn of God, he did choose Judas to
be the one. Saint John tells us: "For Jesus knew from the
beginning which of his followers did not trust him and
who was the man who would betray him. Then he added,
"This is why I said to you, no one can come to me unless
my Father puts it into his heart to come.' As a conse-
quence of this, many of his disciples withdrew and no
longer followed him. So Jesus said to the twelve, 'And are
you too wanting to go away?' 'Lord,' answered Simon
Peter, 'who else should we go to? Your words have the
ring of eternal life! And we believe and are convinced that
you are the Holy One of God.' Jesus replied, 'Did I not
choose you twelve—and one of you has the devil in his
heart.' He was speaking of Judas, the son of Simon Iscariot, one of the twelve, who was planning to betray
him" (John 6:64–71, Phillips).

Jesus then had to live for his entire ministry with this

traitor in his bosom. As he shared his intimate hopes and dreams he was constantly aware of Judas's eyes and the machinations of Judas's mind. Did Jesus try to save Judas? Did he know he had to sleep with this irreverent man next to him? Judas ruined more than Jesus' last supper. From the beginning, Judas stuck into Christ like a knife.

DeQuincey and others have popularized the view that Judas betrayed Jesus in order to force Him to exercise His militant messianic power. This view, which would excuse Judas with a good motive, won't work. Obviously, Judas is no monster, and there is mystery about his treachery. But there is something familiar about his action that everyone should recognize: first getting next to Christ, getting in good with him, and then letting him down, selling him short. If there had been no Judas, one huge aspect of our depravity would never have been represented.

The gospel headlines the evil of Judas's action when Luke declares: "Then entered Satan into Judas surnamed Iscariot . . ." (Luke 22:3, KJV). Jesus said a hard thing about Judas: " 'It is true that the Son of Man will follow the road foretold by the scriptures, but alas for the man through whom he is betrayed! It would be better for that man if he had never been born.' And Judas, who actually betrayed him, said, 'Master, surely I am not the one?' 'You have said it!' replied Jesus" (Matt. 26:24–25, Phillips).

Another aspect of Judas's character that is overlooked by those who would like Judas to appear innocent is that he was a thief and quite money-oriented. Do not forget this passage: "Mary took a whole pound of very expensive perfume, pure nard, and anointed Jesus' feet and then wiped them with her hair. . . . But one of his disciples, Judas Iscariot (the man who was going to betray Jesus), burst out, 'Why on earth wasn't this perfume sold? It's worth thirty pounds, which could have been given to the poor!' He said this, not because he cared about the poor, but because he was dishonest, and when he was in charge of the purse used to help himself from the contents. But Jesus replied to this outburst, 'Let her alone, she has saved this for the day of my burial. You have the poor with you always—you will not always have me!' " (John 12:3–8, Phillips).

"After [Mary's anointing] one of the twelve, Judas Iscariot by name, approached the chief priests. 'What will you give me,' he said to them, 'if I hand him over to you?' They settled with him for thirty silver coins, and from then on he looked for a convenient opportunity to betray Jesus" (Matt. 26:14–16, Phillips). Those coins represented the price of a slave or four months' wages.

What was going through Jesus' mind concerning Judas? Jesus' words, "It were better that this man had never lived," burn in the mind. Were they Jesus' final words on Judas? There is more to it than that.

During supper, according to John, "He then lying on Jesus' breast saith unto him, 'Lord, who is it?' Jesus answered, 'He it is, to whom I shall give a sop, when I have dipped it.' And when he had dipped the sop, he gave it to Judas Iscariot, the son of Simon" (John 13:25–26, KJV). To do this was an act of friendship. You would do it for someone you love. "And after the sop Satan entered into him. Then said Jesus unto him, 'That thou doest, do quickly.' Now no man at the table knew for what intent he spake this unto him. For some of them thought, because Judas had the bag, that Jesus had said unto him, Buy those things that we have need of against the feast; or, that he should give something to the poor. He then having received the sop went immediately out: and it was night. Therefore, when he was gone out, Jesus said, 'Now is the Son of man glorified . . .' " (John 13:27–31, KJV).

Jesus had to bear the burden of Judas's villainy all alone to the end, and his last act to Judas was a kindness. I do not believe Jesus did it in vain nor simply to rub it in. He had washed Judas's feet. I believe this final act of love had an effect on Judas. Jesus never gave up on this man or on any other.

After supper and prayer in the garden Jesus looked up: " 'Look, here comes my betrayer.' And while the words were still on his lips, Judas, one of the twelve, appeared with a great crowd armed with swords and staves, sent by the chief priests and Jewish elders. (The traitor himself had given them a sign, 'The one I kiss will be the man. Get him!') Without any hesitation he walked up to Jesus. 'Greetings, Master!' he cried and kissed him affectionately. 'Judas, my friend,' replied Jesus, 'why are you here?' Then the others came up, seized hold of Jesus and held him" (Matt. 26:46–50, Phillips).

Thank God the story of Judas does not stop here. It is true that in the Book of Acts Luke leads us to believe that Judas kept the blood money and bought a field in which "his bowels gushed out," "the Field of Blood." (Acts 1:-16–20, RSV).

Unlike Matthew, Luke apparently never learned what Judas did. According to Matthew:

> When Judas, who had betrayed him, saw that Jesus was condemned, he was overcome with remorse. He returned the thirty silver coins to the chief priests and elders, with the words, "I have done wrong—I have betrayed an innocent man to death."
>
> "And what has that got to do with us?" they replied. "That's your affair."
>
> And Judas flung down the silver in the Temple, left and went away and hanged himself. But the chief priests picked up the money and said, "It is not right to put this into the Temple treasury, for it is the price of a man's life." So, after a further consultation, they purchased with it the Potter's Field to be a burial-ground for foreigners, which is why it is called the "Field of Blood" to this day. And so the words of Jeremiah the prophet came true:
>
> > And they took the thirty pieces of silver, the price of him that was priced, whom certain of the children of Israel did price; and they gave them for the potter's field, as the Lord appointed me (Matt. 27:3–10, Phillips).

One thing more. From the Cross came the words: "Father, forgive them; for they know not what they do" (Luke 23:34, RSV). Jesus did not say, "Forgive everyone except Judas." That beautiful word *them* excluded no repentant heart. The betrayal was big, but the one on the cross was bigger still.

IN the fifteenth year of the reign of the Emperor Tiberius
(a year when Pontius Pilate was governor of Judaea. . . .)
                                        —LUKE 3:1–2, *Phillips*

(The following chapter is quoted entirely from the New Testament.)

11 / The Judge Who Sentenced Him

"Then they led Jesus from Caiaphas' presence into the palace. It was now early morning and the Jews themselves did not go into the palace, for fear that they would be contaminated and would not be able to eat the Passover. So Pilate walked out to them and said, 'What is the charge that you are bringing against this man?'

" 'If he were not an evil-doer, we should not have handed him over to you,' they replied.

"To which Pilate retorted, 'Then take him yourselves and judge him according to your law.'

" 'We are not allowed to put a man to death,' replied the Jews (thus fulfilling Christ's prophecy of the method of his own death)" (John 18:28–32, Phillips).

"And [they] began their accusation in these words, 'Here is this man whom we have found corrupting our people, and telling them that it is wrong to pay taxes to Caesar, claiming that he himself is Christ, a king' " (Luke 23:2–3, Phillips).

"Then Pilate said to him, 'Do you not hear how many things they testify against you?' But he gave him no answer, not even to a single charge; so that the governor wondered greatly" (Matt. 27:13–14, RSV).

"Pilate . . . asked whether the man was a Galilean. And when he learned that he belonged to Herod's jurisdiction, he sent him over to Herod, who was himself in Jerusalem at that time. When Herod saw Jesus, he was very glad, for he had long desired to see him, because he had heard about him, and he was hoping to see some sign done by him. So he questioned him. . . . The chief priests and the scribes stood by, vehemently accusing him. And Herod with his soldiers treated him with contempt and mocked him; then, arraying him in gorgeous apparel, he sent him back to Pilate. And Herod and Pilate became friends with each other that very day, for before this they had been at enmity with each other.

"Pilate then called together the chief priests and the rulers and the people, and said to them, 'You brought me this man as one who was perverting the people; and after examining him before you, behold, I did not find this man guilty of any of your charges against him; neither did Herod, for he sent him back to us. Behold, nothing deserving death has been done by him; I will therefore chastise him and release him'" (Luke 23:6–16, RSV).

"So Pilate went back into the palace and called Jesus to him. 'Are you the king of the Jews?' he asked.

" 'Are you asking this of your own accord,' replied

Jesus, 'or have other people spoken to you about me?'

" 'Do you think *I* am a Jew?' replied Pilate. 'It's your people and your chief priests who handed you over to me. What have you done, anyway?'

" 'My kingdom is not founded in this world—if it were, my servants would have fought to prevent my being handed over to the Jews. . . .'

" 'So you are a king, are you?' returned Pilate.

" 'You say that I am a king,' Jesus replied; 'the reason for my birth . . . is to witness to the truth. Every man who loves truth recognizes my voice.'

"To which Pilate retorted, 'What is "truth"?' and went straight out again to the Jews and said:

" 'I find nothing criminal about him at all. But I have an arrangement with you to set one prisoner free at Passover time. Do you wish me then to set free for you the "king of the Jews"?'

"At this they shouted at the top of their voices, 'No, not this man, but Barabbas!' " (John 18:33–40, Phillips).

"And among the rebels in prison, who had committed murder in the insurrection, there was a man called Barabbas" (Mark 15:7, RSV).

"So when they had gathered, Pilate said to them, 'Whom do you want me to release for you, Barabbas or Jesus who is called Christ?' For he knew that it was out of envy that they had delivered him up. Besides, while he was sitting on the judgment seat, his wife sent word to him, 'Have nothing to do with that righteous man, for I have suffered much over him today in a dream' " (Matt. 27:17–19, RSV).

"But the chief priests stirred up the crowd to have him release for them Barabbas instead" (Mark 15:11, RSV).

"Then Pilate took Jesus and had him flogged, and the soldiers twisted thorn-twigs into a crown and put it on his head, threw a purple robe around him and kept coming into his presence, saying, 'Hail, king of the Jews!' And then they slapped him with their open hands.

"Then Pilate went outside again and said to them, 'Look, I bring him out before you here, to show that I find nothing criminal about him at all.'

"And at this Jesus came outside too, wearing the thorn crown and the purple robe.

" 'Look,' said Pilate, 'here's the man!'

"The sight of him made the chief priests and Jewish officers shout at the top of their voices, 'Crucify! Crucify!'

" 'You take him and crucify him,' retorted Pilate, 'He's no criminal as far as I can see!'

"The Jews answered him, 'We have a Law, and according to that Law, he must die, for he made himself out to be Son of God!'

"When Pilate heard them say this, he became much more uneasy, and returned to the palace and again spoke to Jesus, 'Where *do* you come from?'

"But Jesus gave him no reply. So Pilate said to him: 'Won't you speak to me? Don't you realize that I have the power to set you free, and I have the power to have you crucified?'

" 'You have no power at all against me,' replied Jesus, 'except what was given to you from above. And for that reason the one who handed me over to you is even more guilty than you are.'

"From that moment, Pilate tried hard to set him free but the Jews were yelling, 'If you set this man free, you are no friend of Caesar! Anyone who makes himself out to be a king is anti-Caesar!'

"When Pilate heard this, he led Jesus outside and sat down upon the Judgment-seat in the place called the Pavement (in Hebrew, Gabbatha). It was the preparation day of the Passover and it was now about midday. Pilate now said to the Jews, 'Look, here's your king!'

"At which they yelled, 'Take him away, take him away, crucify him!'

" 'Am I to crucify your king?' Pilate asked them.

" 'Caesar is our king and no one else,' replied the chief priests" (John 19:1–16, Phillips).

"They were urgent, demanding with loud cries that he should be crucified. And their voices prevailed" (Luke 23:23, RSV).

"So when Pilate saw that he was gaining nothing, but rather that a riot was beginning, he took water and washed his hands before the crowd, saying, 'I am innocent of this man's blood; see to it yourselves.' And all the people answered, 'His blood be on us and on our children!' " (Matt. 27:24–25, RSV).

"And at this Pilate handed Jesus over to them for crucifixion.

"So they took Jesus and he went out carrying the cross himself, to a place called Skull Hill (in Hebrew, Golgotha). There they crucified him, and two others, one on either side of him with Jesus in the middle. Pilate had a placard written out and put on the cross, reading, JESUS OF NAZARETH, THE KING OF THE JEWS. This placard was read by many of the Jews because the place where Jesus was crucified was quite near Jerusalem, and it was written in Hebrew as well as in Latin and Greek. So the chief priests said to Pilate, 'You should not write "The King of the Jews," but "This man said, I am King of the Jews".'

"To which Pilate retorted, 'What I have written, I have written' " (John 19:16–22, Phillips).

"After it was all over, Joseph (who came from Arimathaea and was a disciple of Jesus, though secretly for fear of the Jews) . . ." (John 19:38, Phillips). ". . . took courage and went to Pilate, and asked for the body of Jesus. And Pilate wondered if he were already dead; and summoning the centurion, he asked him whether he was already dead. And when he learned from the centurion that he was dead, he granted the body to Joseph. And he bought a linen shroud, and taking him down, wrapped him in the linen shroud, and laid him in a tomb which had been hewn out of the rock . . ." (Mark 15:43–46, RSV).

"Nicodemus also, the man who had come to him at the beginning by night, arrived bringing a mixture of myrrh and aloes, weighing about a hundred pounds" (John 19:-39, Phillips).

"Mary Magdalene and Mary the mother of Joses saw where he was laid" (Mark. 15:47, RSV).

"Next day, that is, after the day of Preparation, the chief priests and the Pharisees gathered before Pilate and said, 'Sir, we remember how that imposter said, while he was still alive, "After three days I will rise again." Therefore order the sepulchre to be made secure until the third day, lest his disciples go and steal him away, and tell the people, "He has risen from the dead," and the last fraud will be worse than the first.' Pilate said to them, 'You have a guard of soldiers; go, make it as secure as you can.' So they went and made the sepulchre secure by sealing the stone and setting a guard" (Matt. 27:62–66, RSV).

[But Jesus broke through stone and sentry.]

"Some of the guard went into the city and told the chief priests all that had taken place. And when they had assembled with the elders and taken counsel, they gave a sum of money to the soldiers and said, 'Tell people, "His disciples came by night and stole him away while we were asleep." And if this comes to the governor's ears, we will satisfy him and keep you out of trouble.' So they took the money and did as they were directed; and this story has been spread among the Jews to this day" (Matt. 28:11–15, RSV).

ONE day the people were crowding closely round Jesus to hear God's message, as he stood on the shore of Lake Gennesaret. Jesus noticed two boats drawn up on the beach, for the fishermen had left them there while they were cleaning their nets. He went aboard one of the boats, which belonged to Simon, and asked him to push out a little from the shore. Then he sat down and continued his teaching of the crowds from the boat.

When he had finished speaking, he said to Simon, "Push out now into deep water and let down your nets for a catch."

Simon replied, "Master! We've worked all night and never caught a thing, but if you say so, I'll let the nets down."

And when they had done this, they caught an enormous shoal of fish—so big that the nets began to tear. So they signalled to their partners in the other boat to come and help them. They came and filled both the boats to sinking point. When Simon Peter saw this, he fell at Jesus' knees and said,

"Keep away from me, Lord, for I'm only a sinful man!"

For he and his companions (including Zebedee's sons, James and John, Simon's partners) were staggered at the haul of fish they had made.

Jesus said to Simon, "Don't be afraid, Simon. From now on your catch will be *men*."

So they brought the boats ashore, left everything and followed him.

—LUKE 5:1–11, *Phillips*

12 / His Successor

The character Jesus picked for his successor appeared to be the worst possible choice. If anyone then had been asked to pick out which of the twelve disciples might crucify Jesus, Simon Peter might have come to mind long before Judas. It should give us hope that Jesus would entrust his kingdom to this blundering, unstable man.

What is thought to be the stone hut of Simon the fisherman was pointed out to me half-buried in the banks of the Sea of Galilee. The building was about the size of a stall. In which corner did Peter's mother-in-law stay? No wonder she ran a fever. Did Peter clean his fish inside? Where else could he clean the fish smell off? Or did he? To think that the impulsive illiterate man who lived there, or somewhere nearby, became Jesus' lead man! Might that not be enough to encourage anyone else to think Jesus could love him too as beautiful being?

Everyone who writes in the New Testament features Simon. Matthew, Mark, Luke, and John all depict Simon standing next to Christ, with more lines to say and more things to do than all the other disciples together. In the

Bible he leads every list of the twelve, and takes over the command after Christ is finished. Simon was the chief figure in Christ's inner circle, the only disciple who had what it took to stay within hearing distance the day Christ was tried, the first disciple to see Christ after he was "crucified, dead and buried." If there is anyone who would like to meet the Master, it is Simon, son of Jonah, prince of the apostles.

One bright day on the beach of Lake Gennesaret, the congregation crowded so close to Jesus that when it came time to preach his sermon he boarded a boat that belonged to Simon, a fellow follower of John the Baptist. Jesus had Simon back the boat off a bit to give him a moat's breathing space from the congestion, and then took a seat in the bow as his pulpit.

After the benediction, Jesus suggested to Simon that they go fishing out in deep water. The exhausted extrovert shot back testily: "Master, we have toiled all night and caught nothing." But he relented to humor his friend's whim: "At your word I will let down the nets" (Luke 5:5, paraphrase). Immediately the boat sagged with the weight of such an enormous shoal of fish that the nets began to rip. They had to signal frantically for help to their partners in the other boat. The sons of Zebedee arrived just in time to help land the catch. Both boats were filled so high with fish that the water was dangerously near the gunwales.

The story is told to describe the effect it had on Simon, who believed it to be more than good luck. According to Luke, this incredible catch shook out of Simon a shockingly lovely prayer. It was shocking because it was the first prayer he had ever said, and the first that others had ever heard said at the feet of another man: "Depart from me, for I am a sinful man, O Lord" (Luke 5:8, RSV).

And then came what must have been a very special moment in Simon's life. In what Pharisees would dismiss as an informal service of ordination, all hands standing by on the tossing deck of the little ship, Jesus, swaying over Simon, personally delivered to Simon his holy orders: "Do not be afraid; henceforth you will be catching men" (Luke 5:10, RSV). According to Luke, the other four sailors suddenly repeated their vows with astonishing results: "And when they had brought their boats to land, they left everything and followed him" (Luke 5:11, RSV).

Not long after Jesus discovered Simon, Simon discovered Jesus. We marvel yet over Christ's eye for choosing men. What would we have done without this fisherman who was able to identify Christ? The teacher did not have much time and could put off their examination no longer.

"But who do you say that I am?" (Luke 9:20, RSV). Everything depended on someone getting that answer right. We often ponder what it required to be Christ. Think for a moment about what it took for a man to recognize Christ. The average man does not see that well. This perspective would require more of a miracle than producing a shoal of fish.

Men hung on Jesus' words. Surely that day he hung on theirs. We do not know how long he had to wait. We only know that he had to wait until someone knew him well enough to introduce him to the rest of the world. Suddenly, the shining answer that the ages had sought fell like light on the eyes of the son of Jonah. It is a moment not to be taken lightly. For this rough seaman was the first ever to recognize the face of Jesus as the face of the Son of God. John had baptized Jesus; now it was Simon's turn to knight him with "the name that is above every other name," and still is to this day. Was he choked, hoarse with emotion? From somewhere the words came: "You are . . . Christ . . ." (Matt. 16:16, RSV).

Something about this passage makes us think Christ's eyes were wet as he turned to bless the big man who named him. In return, he gave Simon a new name. Simon had called Jesus, "Christ." Christ now called Simon, "Rock" (Matt. 16:18, RSV). *Rock* in Greek is *petra,* which is close to the Greek *Petros,* or Peter. The Master was resting the kingdom on the Gibraltar of Peter's faith.

Peter missed the next question. After making a perfect answer, he made a terrible blunder. Peter was determined to make the Messiah king, but Christ confessed He must suffer and die for a different crown. Peter could not understand it: "Peter took him and began to rebuke him, saying: 'God forbid, Lord!' " (Matt. 16:22, RSV). For Christ, the decision was so difficult that he came down hard on his hard-headed pilgrim: "Get behind me, Satan! You are a hindrance to me; for you are not on the side of God, but of men" (Matt 16:23, RSV). Jesus tried to explain, "If any man would come after me, let him deny himself and take up his cross and follow me" (Matt. 16:- 24, RSV). It was difficult since the Rock was hard to move. It would be some time before Peter could say: "Lo, we have left everything and followed you" (Mark 10:28, RSV).

About a week later, Jesus appointed Peter to be one of the three to go up to the mountain with him to pray. And on that summit Peter saw something that registered. Peter later told Mark that during the Master's prayer something overwhelming took place. They saw it first in Christ's face, but then the light fell all over him until he was so transfigured it was frightening. Then Christ conferred with Moses and Elijah. Dashing in where angels fear to tread, Peter interrupted to propose that they make a shrine for each. A voice emanating from a cloud put Peter in his place, saying, "This is my beloved Son; listen to him" (Mark 9:7, RSV). Peter did not argue again about the Son's divine right to reign his way. He was learning what the prophet meant by a suffering servant. Jesus was not going to campaign from a snow-white steed, but would be without a horse and weaponless. "He was bruised for our iniquities; . . . and with his stripes we are healed" (Isa. 53:5, RSV).

When the time came to set the table for the last time, Jesus turned to Peter and John to prepare it, though Peter nearly ruined that last evening for Him. It was a night to remember—and to forget. Peter did everything wrong. At first he refused to let Jesus wash his feet; then he wanted a bath. At suppertime Jesus made an announcement that sank every heart: "Believe me, one of you is going to betray me—someone who is now eating with me" (Mark 14:18, Phillips).

Peter made more trouble when he boasted vehemently: "Lord, why cannot I follow thee now? I will lay down my life for thy sake" (John 13:37, KJV). Jesus stated that Peter would disown him thrice before the cock crowed twice.

Later, in the garden, when Jesus' heart was breaking, he asked Peter several times as a special favor to pray for him. Peter took a nap. Then, when Judas crept up to kiss Christ good-bye, Peter cut off a soldier's ear, an act that would have started a fight fatal to the plan had Jesus not been there to heal the injured man. And then the Rock skipped out with the rest, leaving the One to whom he had sworn eternal allegiance alone to face the end.

Later that night, Peter pulled himself together and tried to follow Christ once more, but from a safe distance. He found the nerve to work his way to the high priest's court to view the disaster. He heard them spit. He saw Christ struck, heard the cries from the crowd, and saw the three crosses.

While Peter was warming himself at a charcoal fire and trying to look nonchalant, a girl pointed her finger at him: "This man also was with him."

Peter snapped back: "Woman, I do not know him."

Next he ran into the companion of the man whose ear he had cut off. "You also are one of them," he said.

"No," Peter shouted. A little later his Galilean accent gave him away, but he swore he didn't even know about whom they were talking. "The next thing Peter knew, a cock was crowing and he was crying uncontrollably" (Luke 22:54–62, paraphase).

Jesus descended into hell, as did Peter. Judas killed

himself, suffering only once, but Peter must have tortured
himself by dying a thousand deaths in those three dark
days. He could not bear to live, but neither could he die.
An angel must have held back his dagger hand, while
another rolled back a stone and spoke such fantastic
words to Mary that she flew with news to Peter. Peter
could not run as fast as John, but he was the next to burst
into the vacant tomb where John waited. That discovery
delivered Peter from his living death, and turned his crying shame into a sermon that the power at Pentecost used
to convert three thousand people.

After that, the gates of hell could not stop the big
fisherman. He straightened a cripple's legs on his way to
church. Using his new power Peter made his way out of
jail without breaking a lock, except on the warden's heart.
He broke out of the Jewish dietary restrictions to get
ready for Paul to export the message to the whole world.
When you think of yourself as beyond hope remember
what Jesus did with Peter.

When the authorities warned Peter to stop his subver-
sive propaganda about a dead carpenter, he stood fast:
"Whether it is right in the eyes of God for us to listen to
what you say rather than to what he says, you must
decide; for we cannot help speaking about what we have
actually seen and heard!" (Acts 4:19–20, Phillips). Luke
said that people so admired Peter that they bowed before
him against his will, and that when he was expected to
take a certain route, people would haul the sick into the
streets in hopes that his shadow might fall upon them in
healing blessing (Acts 5:15, paraphrase).

Saint John remembers a moving conversation that took place between Peter and the newly risen Lord. "Jesus said to Simon Peter, 'Simon, son of John, do you love me more than these?' [Peter] said to him, 'Yes, Lord; you know that I love you.' He said to him, 'Feed my lambs.' A second time he said to him, 'Simon, son of John, do you love me?' He said to him, 'Yes, Lord; you know that I love you.' He said to him, 'Tend my sheep.' He said to him the third time, 'Simon, son of John, do you love me?' Peter was grieved . . ." perhaps for the other three times when he had denied Jesus. But these three times he admitted he knew Christ with all his heart. " 'Lord, you know everything; you know that I love you.' Jesus said to him, 'Feed my sheep' " (John 21:15–17, RSV). The church stands as proof he kept his promise.

Christ was not mistaken in his man. If Peter had failed at first, he made up for it in the end. It is said that when it came Peter's turn to be nailed to the cross in the gritting teeth of Nero's Rome, his last request was that he die head down, for he felt he was not worthy to die upright as Christ had. Surely this made him worthy of the words of Him who had said, "Upon this rock I will build my church; and the gates of hell shall not prevail against it" (Matt. 16:18, KJV).